HOW THE FEET...

Missionary Stories
Family Devotionals

Written By:
Stacey L. Clemento

Faithful Life Publishers
Sebring, FL 33870

FaithfulLifePublishers.com
info@FaithfulLifePublishers.com
888.720.0950

The author's picture on the back cover was provided by Shaun Reilly Photography, 609-318-4768.

All references come from the King James Version.

The writings and teachings of this publication are presented by the author and do not necessarily reflect or represent the views, beliefs or opinions held by Faithful Life Publishers.

28 27 26 25   1 2 3 4 5

Table of Contents

Gladys Aylward

Missionary to China

Day 1: Gladys Aylward part 1

Bible Truth: God will direct our paths according to His will.

Gladys Aylward. A true hero and lady of faith. She would have never dreamed of the journey, accomplishments, and impact that her life would have on others due to her trust and unfailing confidence in Jesus Christ. Yet God knew the great plans He had for Gladys. Plans to show his goodness, love, and redeeming power to others across the world.

Gladys started life as a very poor parlor maid of small stature. At the age of 26, she attended a revival meeting where the preacher spoke on dedicating one's life to the service of God. Gladys responded to the message and felt God's calling on her life to fulltime missionary work in China. Gladys enrolled in the China Inland Mission's Center. However, she failed to pass the examinations to be a missionary that the China Inland Mission's Center would support. She was told she did not have what it would take to be a missionary to China and would never be able to learn the difficult language. Still, Gladys was determined, and in her heart knew that God called her to China. She would not let men persuade her to give up on the calling of God in her life, regardless of the challenges. And if China was where God wanted, God would have to be the one to direct her path to get her there.

Truth Verse(s): Proverbs 16:9, Jeremiah 29:11 & Ephesians 2:10

Day 2: Bible Discussion

Bible Truth: God will direct our paths according to His will.

Truth Verse(s): Proverbs 16:9, Jeremiah 29:11 & Ephesians 2:10

Bible Lesson: Read Genesis 12:1-2, 13:16, 15:1-4, 16:1-4, 17:1-4, 18:10-11, 21:1-3

God had a plan for Abraham. But just like Gladys, it was all up to God to get him there.

God called Abraham from his father's house to one day be a great nation in the promised land. As Abraham and his wife Sarah journeyed, many years passed. Still, God had not given Abraham and Sarah a child. They trusted God, but some days it was hard, just like it was for Gladys when she was rejected from the China Inland Mission Center. But Abraham and Sarah continued pressing forward, just like Gladys, because they knew where God called them. Abraham and Sarah even tried to help God out with the child by Abraham taking Sarah's maid Hagar to wife. Still, that was not God's will for the promised seed of Abraham. Finally, when Abraham was over 99 years old, the Lord visited Sarah and allowed her to conceive. Sarah gave birth shortly after to Isaac, the promised seed of Abraham.

Both Gladys and Abraham trusted God and held his promises as true. Regardless of the difficult circumstances, challenges, or just how impossible the situation may appear to us, God will always make a way for His will to be accomplished.

Thought: Is God calling you to something that requires trust?

Day 3: Gladys Aylward part 2

Bible Truth: The Lord is always good, and He will meet your needs.

Gladys trusted God's calling on her life to be a missionary. It was clear that the mission center was not going to provide financially for Gladys to reach China. God would have to provide the funds. God opened opportunities that allowed her to work and save for her trip. Gladys learned of a veteran missionary woman named Mrs. Jeannie Lawson, who needed help with her work on the mission field in China. Gladys was thrilled at the opportunity. It would not be an easy journey though as Gladys could not afford to travel by ship, only by train. Gladys was not at all concerned about what little she had as her journey began. She trusted the Lord to meet her needs. She pressed on with one suitcase filled with food and clothes and a mere 2 pounds.

Gladys traveled the Trans-Siberian Railway. However, her train trip took her straight into a war zone. The Russian Chinese war raged. The Russian conductor of the train shouted at Gladys in words she did not understand. Gladys could tell by his voice and angry face that she was being forced off the train. With gunfire, snow, and frigid cold temperatures, Gladys walked thirty miles back to the nearest city. She faced starvation, freezing to death, and being forced temporarily into the Soviet military. Gladys fully trusted God through the difficult journey.

Truth Verse(s): Romans 8:28 and Psalms 112:7

Day 4: Bible Discussion

Bible Truth: The Lord is always good, and He will meet your needs.

Truth Verse(s): Romans 8:28 and Psalms 112:7

Bible Lesson: Read Numbers 13:1-2, 13:28-33, 14:6-8, 14:33-34, Deuteronomy 8:2-4, Deuteronomy 8:7-10

God had promised to give the Israelites a land flowing with milk and honey. The day came where God commanded Moses to send spies to search out the Promised Land. The land was truly good, just as God had promised. However, ten of the twelve spies brought back an evil report due to fear of the other nations in the land. Caleb and Joshua trusted God was calling them to that Promised Land, just like Gladys trusted God's calling for her to go to China. As a result of the rebellion, God had the Israelites wander in the wilderness for forty years. Gladys had a difficult trip to get to where God called her and now the Israelites would face difficulty too. But as Gladys trusted God to provide for her along the journey, God provided for Israel too. God fed them manna, gave them water from a rock, and their clothes never wore out.

The Israelites kept moving to where God had called them, just as Gladys did as she journeyed to China. And God met the need of both the Israelites and Gladys all along the way because He is good, all the time.

Thought: Is there something you need to trust God to provide?

Day 5: Gladys Aylward part 3

Bible Truth: God is love and we can show His love to others by working hard and meeting the needs of others.

Gladys eventually reached Vladivostok, Russia, then sailed to Japan before finally reaching Tientsin, China. She then took a train, bus, and a mule to the inland city of Yangchen. It was here that Gladys met Mrs. Lawson. Yangchen was a very popular caravan stop. The two women had a wonderful idea to open an inn at Yangchen so they could better tell the travelers about Jesus and salvation. The ladies set out with much hard work and sweat ahead of them. And so was the beginning of "The Inn of the Sixth Happiness".

The Inn was now ready for travelers to stop and stay and hear about Jesus. But there was a problem. No one would come. Day after day caravans would stroll in but would avoid stopping at the inn. Gladys had to get creative. She knew the mules in caravans understood that turning into the inn of a courtyard meant food, water, and rest. So, Gladys intercepted the lead mule in a caravan and led it directly into her inn's courtyard. The rest of the caravan followed. The muleteers received good food, warm beds, and free entertainment as the Innkeepers told stories about Jesus and His cross at Calvary. Gladys took great care of her guests and soon no longer had to kidnap customers. Over the weeks, some of the muleteers learned of their need for a Savior. Christianity began to spread as the muleteers retold the stories of Jesus as they journeyed on their way.

Truth Verse(s): 1 John 4:7-8 and James 1:22

Day 6: Bible Discussion

Bible Truth: God is love and gives us opportunities to show His love to others by working hard and meeting the needs.

Truth Verse(s): 1 John 4:7-8 and James 1:22

Bible Lesson: Acts 9:36-42

Dorcas, also known as Tabitha, was a disciple of Jesus Christ who lived in Joppa. Tabitha was full of good works. She went about doing good for others to show and share the love of Jesus Christ, just like Gladys and Mrs. Lawson at the "Inn of Sixth Happiness". Tabitha became very sick and died. The widows put Tabitha in an upper room and the disciples called for Peter. When Peter arrived, the weeping widows showed Peter the coats and garments that Tabitha had made them. God gave Tabitha opportunities to serve others by meeting their needs. The widows, as well as many others, were not only able to see first-hand the miracle of Tabitha being brought back to life, but because such a crowd had gathered due to the love these widows had for Tabitha, many believed on Jesus Christ and were saved.

Gladys and Mrs. Lawson worked hard to meet the needs of food and shelter, showing love, which drew a crowd. And as a result, many muleteers would hear God's Word and be saved.

Thought: Is there something you can do for someone else to meet a need and show the love and compassion of Christ? It just might open the door for someone to get saved!

Day 7: Gladys Aylward part 4

Bible Truth: God will promote those who are faithful and humble.

The sad day came when Mrs. Lawson died and the work of the Inn was left to Gladys and Yang, the Chinese Christian who was the cook at the "Inn of Sixth Happiness". Gladys was becoming quite popular among the Chinese people and soon the Mandarin of Yangchen himself came to pay Gladys a visit. The Mandarin had an important job for Gladys. It had been a long custom in the Chinese culture to bind the feet of girls from the time they were infants to prevent their feet from growing. This custom caused the women to have extremely tiny feet. Binding the feet forced women to walk with slow, tottering steps, which was looked upon as graceful. However, the practice was very painful for the infants and girls as they grew with bound feet. The practice was finally considered inhumane, and the practice of foot binding was to be outlawed. The government needed someone, preferably a woman, who could travel and enforce the new law. The Mandarin called upon Gladys for the job, and she became the official foot inspector appointed by the Mandarin himself. This would present a new opportunity for Gladys to travel to several other areas as the official foot inspector, opening the door for her to share salvation through Jesus Christ with more people that she would have never reached at the "Inn of Sixth Happiness".

Truth Verse(s): Luke 19:17 and Psalm 75:6-7

Day 8: Bible Discussion

Bible Truth: God will promote those who are faithful and humble.

Truth Verse(s): Luke 19:17 and Psalm 75:6-7

Bible Lesson: Read Genesis 41:28-44

Joseph was sold into slavery in Egypt by his own brothers. Eventually, Joseph was thrown into prison for a crime he didn't commit. However, Joseph remained faithful and continued to be a servant of God, even in the prison. Joseph desired to be a good testimony for the Lord. Eventually, Pharaoh had a dream which troubled him. It was told Pharaoh that a man in the prison could interpret dreams. Pharaoh called for Joseph to be brought forward. God revealed the dreams to Joseph, and he was able to interpret them for Pharaoh. God gave Joseph wisdom to share with Pharaoh as how to overcome the soon to be famine in Egypt. Pharaoh was impressed with Joseph and made him second in command in all of Egypt, just under Pharaoh himself.

Just as God was with Joseph and brought him a promotion, the Lord did the same for Gladys. He promoted Gladys to a new role, working as a Chinese government official, which allowed her to share the gospel with a broader population in China. Gladys was faithful with the little "Inn of Sixth Happiness" and as a result, God saw fit to give her more.

Thought: Is there something God has for you to do, no matter how small, that you can be faithful with, so He can trust you with more?

Day 9: Gladys Aylward part 5

Bible Truth: God will never leave us nor forsake us, even in the face of danger. We do not need to fear.

Gladys performed her new job well and that impressed the Mandarin. It was during her second year in Yangchen, Gladys was summoned by the Mandarin again. This time, he had a very dangerous assignment for Gladys. This assignment would test not only her faith but would be a living example of God's power. This would require Gladys to show trust and faith in God as her life would be on the line. The Mandarin had informed Gladys that a riot had broken out with the men in the local prison. The prisoners were attacking and killing each other in a violent rage. The Mandarin demanded that Gladys go into the prison and stop the rioting. Yes, small, petite Gladys. Gladys knew her God was big and that her eternal salvation was secure. She could find rest in her Savior, even in the face of death. The Mandarin told Gladys he heard her teach that those who trusted in her God had nothing to fear. Therefore, Gladys was the one to go into the prison and stop the riot. Gladys knew this would be a make-or-break point in the Chinese seeing her powerful God's hand at work or not. This would be an amazing victory in winning the Chinese people to Christ. Gladys, scared but brave, trusted the Lord to show up and fight for her. She took a deep breath as she slowly headed into the midst of the prison riot.

Truth Verse(s): Psalm 118:6, Psalm 56:3, and Joshua 1:9

Day 10: Bible Discussion

Bible Truth: God will never leave us nor forsake us, even in the face of danger. We do not need to fear.

Truth Verse(s): Psalm 118:6, Psalm 56:3 and Joshua 1:9

Bible Lesson: Read Daniel 3:12-25

Shadrach, Meshach, and Abednego refused to bow down and worship the golden statue of King Nebuchadnezzar. This made the king very angry. He gave them one final chance to bow down to the statue or they would be cast into the fiery furnace. They responded with full faith and trust in their Lord. The three young Hebrews responded that even if God did not save them from the fiery furnace, they would still trust that He would deliver them from the king's hand. They chose to go through the fire, trusting God for the outcome, and hoping to be used as a testimony for the Lord for all to see. God went with them into the fiery furnace, saved them, and showed just how powerful He truly was in the lives of those who have faith in Him.

Just as the three young Hebrews had faith as they faced the fiery furnace, trusting the hand of their Redeemer, Gladys was tested to show the same faith. Although she was not faced with a fiery furnace, she faced her own death sentence as she boldly decided to trust God and show just how powerful He was, using a very small woman to intervene in a men's prison riot.

Thought: Is there something that causes you fear, but you know you need to stand for truth for God's power to shine?

Day 11: Gladys Aylward part 6

Bible Truth: God will deliver you from trouble when you trust in Him.

Gladys prayed as the prison doors opened and she walked in. Gladys needed God's grace and mercy. The scene was unimaginable. People screaming and running for their lives. Bodies lay dead everywhere. A man ran straight towards Gladys with a machete screaming as he came near. Gladys shouted, "stop and drop that weapon". It worked! The man stopped and put down the weapon. She then yelled, "quiet" and was able to restore order. One appointed spokesperson could now speak on behalf of the prisoners. Gladys wanted to find out what caused the riot. Gladys listened to the men and then assured them she would discuss the issues with the Mandarin. Gladys left the prison and spoke with the Mandarin. She told him the men were bored and over-crowded in the prison. There was not enough food or clothing. Gladys suggested work for the prisoners, looms to make clothes and grindstones to make grain. They could make what they needed for the prisoners and sell the rest to raise money for the prison. She was given the name "ai-weh-deh" which meant Virtuous One. God gave Gladys wisdom to help transform the prison to be a better place. She supplied the prisoners with Bibles. God used the faith and trust of one small woman in danger, to show his power and bring prisoners to a saving knowledge of Jesus Christ.

Truth Verse(s): Psalm 50:15 and I John 5:14

Day 12: Bible Discussion

Truth: God can deliver you from trouble when you trust in Him.

Truth Verse(s): Psalm 50:15 and I John 5:14

Bible Story: Daniel 6:13-23

King Darius made a decree that no one should pray to any god except him. Daniel was a Jew and believed in the one true God in heaven. Therefore, he did not obey the decree but continued to pray three times a day. Some other men in the kingdom who wanted Daniel's position, told King Darius about Daniel, and reminded him that the decree could not be changed. King Darius was upset he made the decree, but nevertheless, delivered Daniel to be thrown into the lion's den. A stone was placed to seal the den. Daniel prayed to God for help during this time of danger in his life. God sent angels to shut the mouths of the lions and no harm came to Daniel. The King returned the next morning to find Daniel alive and well and had him lifted from the den. Daniel proclaimed the great wonders God had done for him in the den and God's power was displayed for all to see.

God was with Daniel in his great time of trouble in his life, just as God was with Gladys. God protected Gladys from harm as she entered that prison, just as He did Daniel in the lion's den. God will hear our cry in times of trouble, and He is able to deliver us, should that be His will…when we trust in Him.

Thought: Is there trouble or fear in your life you need to give to God and trust Him to see you through?

Day 13: Gladys Aylward part 7

Bible Truth: Those who are faithful and diligent in the small things will be rewarded from God with more.

Gladys now had the ministry and care of the Inn of the Sixth Happiness as well as the prison ministry as a result of her help with the prison riot. However, God had yet another new and exciting opportunity awaiting Gladys. It was not long after the prison ministry that God opened the doors of this new adventure in ministry for Gladys. One day while Gladys was out in town, she had noticed a beggar woman by the road. Alongside of the beggar woman was a very dirty, malnourished child, who appeared sick. Gladys was overcome with great compassion for the child. God gave Gladys discernment to realize the child did not belong to the beggar woman and Gladys offered to buy the little girl. Gladys paid nine pence for the girl, who was about age five. The name, "Nine pence" seemed to fit, so that is what Gladys named the little girl. "Nine pence" was brought back to the Inn of the Sixth Happiness to live with Gladys and Yang. Not long after, Ninepence came home with a small orphan boy. She told Gladys that she would eat less so the boy could stay and have something to eat too. The Aylward clan began to grow. And so began a new area of ministry for Gladys; that she would be a mother to orphaned children.

Truth Verse(s): Matthew 25:21 and Colossians 3:24

Day 14: Bible Discussion

Bible Truth: Those who are faithful and diligent will be rewarded.

Truth Verse(s): Matthew 25:21 and Colossians 3:24

Bible Lesson: Read Matthew 25:14-30

Jesus told a parable of the unfaithful servant. He explained how the master entrusted his goods to his servants while he was away. He would return later to collect his goods as well as what was gained. Two of the three servants had done well in using the talents their master lent to them to gain more for the master when he returned. The master was pleased when he returned and rewarded them with "well done good and faithful servant". One of the servants, however, did not use the talents given to him to produce more. Instead, the unfaithful servant buried the talent given to him from his master. Therefore, the master took the talent from the wicked servant and gave it to the servant with ten talents. Jesus explained that those who are faithful with what He gives them, will be entrusted and given more.

Gladys was busy doing the work of the Lord. God gave Gladys more opportunities to minister and reach others for Jesus Christ because she was willing to use what God had given her previously. As Gladys trusted and willingly served God, He entrusted more to her care.

Thought: Is there a talent God has given you that He desires you to use for his glory? He just may be waiting to give you more if you are faithful in the small things.

Day 15: Gladys Aylward part 8

Bible Truth: As a Christian, we should have a part in the great commission and bringing others to Christ for Salvation.

Gladys continued her regular visits with the Mandarin. He was not a Christian, but he enjoyed the conversations that he and Gladys shared. The two of them had become very good friends. Gladys was given her official Chinese citizenship in 1936. She lived a simple life and blended in well with the culture of China. More than just being a missionary, Gladys had allowed China to become her home. She loved the people of China greatly and they became like family.

In 1938, war broke out with China and Japan. The Japanese bombed the city of Yangchen, where Gladys lived. Many fled or were left dead. Within a few days, the Japanese had seized Yangchen. It was at this time that the Mandarin pleaded for survivors to flee to the mountains. It was at this time that the Mandarin also expressed an interest that he too wanted to become a Christian. He made a profession of his faith in Jesus Christ. The Mandarin had become a new Christian, believing in Jesus Christ to save him from his sins and an eternity in hell. The Mandarin wanted to live his live for Jesus Christ and pointing others to salvation.

Truth Verse(s): I Corinthians 3:6, Mark 16:15, and Acts 1:8

Day 16: Bible Discussion

Bible Truth: As a Christian, we should have a part in the great commission and bringing others to Christ for Salvation.

Truth Verse(s): I Corinthians 3:6, Mark 16:15, and Acts 1:8

Bible Lesson: Read Matthew 13:1-9, 18-23

Jesus told a parable about the sower of the seed. The seed is the Word of God, including the plan of salvation through Jesus Christ alone. This is also known as the gospel or good news. The gospel being shared with others is the great commission. There are times we will sow the Word of God to different people who may or may not be ready to receive what we have to offer. Sometimes people listen quickly but fade away. Other times it is a stony ground, and the Word does not take root at all. Then, there are times the ground may be soft, and the Word of God easily received and accepted by those we are telling about salvation and Jesus. We cannot control the type of ground or heart that we are sharing God's Word with, however, it is still our job to plant and let God give the increase.

Gladys did not grow weary in sharing God's Word and Jesus's plan for salvation with others, especially the Mandarin. She remained faithful to plant and eventually she saw the fruit of the crop planted when the Mandarin became a Christian.

Thought: Are you involved with the great commission? God commands us to share Jesus with a lost world.

Day 17: Gladys Aylward part 9

Bible Truth: God hears our prayers in time of need and will answer.

The war continued in China. The Mandarin took counsel from Gladys on what to do with the many prisoners and the prisoners were released to flee to safety too. News reached Gladys that there was a bounty for the capture of her and the Mandarin. By this time, Gladys had two hundred orphans under her care. She sent one hundred orphans to safety and had the remaining children with her. Gladys set out to reach the orphanage at Sian. They walked for twelve days, sometimes finding shelter with friends, other nights left unprotected in the mountains. After twelve days, they reached the Yellow River. But they found no way to cross. The children asked Gladys if God will help them. They pleaded with her to ask God to make a way for them to cross the river. On the edge of the riverbank, the group gathered, knelt, and prayed. They began to sing to the Lord in Chinese. Just then, an officer heard the singing and approached them. The officer was a Chinese soldier, not Japanese. He made arrangements for Gladys and the children to cross the river safely. God heard their cry, met their need, and the journey continued forward.

Truth Verse(s): I John 5:14 and Micah 7:7

Day 18: Bible Discussion

Truth: God hears our prayers in time of need and will answer.

Truth Verse(s): I John 5:14 and Micah 7:7

Bible Story: Read Exodus 14:10-30

Moses had led the Israelite children out of slavery in Egypt towards the Promised Land. However, God had hardened Pharaoh's heart that he should pursue Moses and the Israelites to bring them again into captivity in Egypt. The Israelites were cornered as the Egyptian army closed in on them. The Israelites had no way to escape with mountains and sea on all sides. They were trapped at the Red Sea with no way to cross. They cried unto Moses for deliverance. Moses sought God for the people and to intercede on their behalf. The Lord told Moses to lift his staff over the Red Sea and He would part the sea, so the Israelites could cross on dry ground. The Lord heard their cry and delivered them from the Egyptian army.

Gladys faced a river that she was not able to cross with the children. They called upon God to help them in their time of need. Although the Lord did not part the river for them, He gave them a miracle in that a Chinese soldier was able to hear them and not a Japanese enemy soldier. In addition, they were not seen and captured from the enemy planes that had flown above. God heard their cry and delivered them safely, just like the Israelites at the Red Sea.

Thought: Has God kept you safe from something that could have gone wrong? Do not overlook his hand of safety each and every day.

Day 19: Gladys Aylward part 10

Bible Truth: Those who will be first in God's kingdom, will be those who serve. And those who are willing to serve, will be greatly used by God.

A difficult journey still lay ahead. The orphanages they reached on the other side of the river were full and the group was turned down, forced to travel further. After more than twenty days of traveling on foot with the orphans, they finally reached an orphanage that could take them in. Gladys, exhausted, collapsed from typhus fever and fell into delirium for several days.

God was not done using Gladys yet. She regained her health and started a church in Sian. Gladys also worked with the lepers near Tibet. Her injuries sustained during the war left her impaired and she had to return to England for medical help. But she did not fully rest as she continued with evangelizing in England. Gladys understood that her mission field was anywhere that God planted her. Soon, she settled in Taiwan and set up another orphanage.

Gladys's life was filled with love for her Savior and a compassion to see others saved, especially the Chinese people whom she had grown to love. She lived to serve her Jesus whole heartedly. She died in 1970 in Taiwan after living an adventurous life serving God and others. Gladys was truly a servant, just like Jesus.

Truth Verse(s): Mark 9:35 and John 12:26

Day 20: Bible Discussion

Bible Truth: Those who will be first in God's kingdom, will be those who serve. Those who are willing to serve, will be greatly used by God.

Truth Verse(s): Mark 9:35 and John 12:26

Bible Story: Read Acts 6:8,15 and Acts 7:54-60 and Acts 8:2

Stephen was a great man of God, who lived to serve others with compassion and love. He desired to serve others just as Jesus, His Savior had done. The Jewish leaders did not like that Stephen preached the gospel about Jesus and sought to have him stoned. Stephen stood bold in his faith, proclaimed the whole truth, and asked God to forgive those who stoned him as He died. Because of Stephen's service and dedication to the Lord, He was greatly missed, and his legacy is read even today, years later, as a testimony of God's goodness and what can be accomplished through those that live and love Christ.

Just as Stephen had a good name and was missed dearly when he died, the same was true for Gladys. She had made such an impact on the lives of the Chinese people and left a godly legacy behind. Both Stephen and Gladys will be first in God's kingdom as they truly served others like Jesus Christ.

Thought: Is your testimony and service for Jesus leaving a godly and positive impact on those around you?

Eric Liddell

Missionary to China

Day 21: Eric Liddell part 1

Bible Truth: God has a plan for each of our lives and will prepare us for those plans.

Eric Liddell was a man who put God first in his life. God gave Eric many talents and gifts, and Eric used those talents and gifts for the glory of the Lord, as he served Jesus Christ. God would use various times in Eric's life to prepare him for the work that the Lord would have him do for the kingdom of God.

Eric was born on the mission field in China in 1902. His parents had been serving Jesus Christ in China by sharing the gospel with the Chinese people through the Siaochang mission station. God used the Siaochang mission station early in Eric's life to grow his love for Jesus and plant seeds to prepare Eric for missions work later in life.

When Eric was only about 5 years old, a group known as the Boxers rose in China and began a period referred to as the Boxer Rebellion. The Boxers were killing foreigners in China, which meant many missionaries were in danger. The Boxers killed about two hundred missionaries during this time. One night when the Boxers attacked, Eric's parents were able to escape and took their three children on a furlough back to Scotland. His parents enrolled Eric and his brother Rob, in a missionary school for boys and soon left to return to China to serve God. It was at this time, the Lord began to show Eric just what his talents were, which God would later use for his glory and to bring others to Christ.

Truth Verse(s): Jeremiah 29:11 and Ephesians 2:10

Day 22: Bible Discussion

Bible Truth: God has a plan for each of our lives and will prepare us for those plans.

Truth Verse(s): Jeremiah 29:11 and Ephesians 2:10

Bible Lesson: Read I Samuel 17:32-50

Just as God had prepared David for his battle with Goliath using a slingshot, God was preparing Eric through situations, talents, and gifts that would later be used for God's glory and ministry. David was a shepherd. A well-known choice weapon of a shepherd was a sling shot. God had David grow up as a shepherd boy, learning and mastering the use of the deadly slingshot while protecting his sheep. David had years of practice as a youth, to learn how to handle such a weapon. Through the job as a shepherd boy while he was young, God was training David to be used in the future. David now had an opportunity to bring glory to God by defeating the giant, Goliath, with a slingshot and stone that sunk deep into Goliath's forehead. The accuracy to hit such a specific, small target area, was the result of the practice that God gave David in the wilderness protecting his sheep. We will soon see exactly what talents God was developing in Eric's life to use later for the glory of God.

Thought: What are the talents, gifts, or interests that God may be preparing in your life, to serve Him in the future?

Day 23: Eric Liddell part 2

Bible Truth: Anything, including good things, can become an idol in our life. Always keep Christ first!

Eric was a well-rounded young man. He excelled not only in the classroom, but also in sports, specifically track. Many people were about to see the God-given talent Eric had for running and just how fast he really was.

In 1920, Eric enrolled at the University of Edinburg. He began to study chemistry, which is something God would also use later in Eric's life. One day, Eric was challenged to race the reigning Scottish champion of running. Eric accepted the challenge. He lost the race that day, but only by inches, which encouraged him to train harder. Eric was making a name for himself as "The Flying Scotsman" and was soon challenged to race Great Britain's fastest athlete. But the end of this day was much different than the first. Eric had not only won the 100 yard and 220-yard dash, but he also set new world records that would not be broken for 35 years.

It was about this time, that Eric's mother encouraged her son to use his talents for Christ. He had the famous, "Flying Scotsman" nickname and this drew attention to himself. Eric was able to use this as an opportunity to speak to people about Jesus Christ. He talked about Christ so much, that many began to question if Eric was more committed to God, or his running. They would soon find out.

Truth Verse(s): I John 5:21 and Exodus 20:3

Day 24: Bible Discussion

Bible Truth: Anything, including good things, can become an idol in our life. Always keep Christ first!

Truth Verse(s): I John 5:21 and Exodus 20:3

Bible Lesson: Read Genesis 22:1-18

God had promised Abraham a son. Years had passed and Abraham had yet to see this promise fulfilled. But when Abraham was one hundred years old, God allowed Sarah to conceive and give birth to a baby boy, named Isaac. Abraham loved Isaac so, but this became a problem. Did Abraham love Isaac more than God? Did Abraham love Isaac more than obedience to God? God would give Abraham a test. Abraham was to take Isaac and sacrifice him as a burnt offering to the Lord. This was a test to see if Abraham was willing to trust God over everything else that mattered to Abraham. Because of Abraham's trust in God's promises, Abraham obeyed God and set out to offer Isaac as a sacrifice. Abraham's obedience displayed that Isaac would not be an idol in the life of Abraham standing between him and God. Abraham passed the test to put God first in everything, even if he did not fully understand. God was pleased to be at the center of Abraham's life. God provided his own ram for a sacrifice instead of Isaac. God could see that Abraham was willing to walk in full surrender and obedience, and not withhold any area of his life from God.

Thought: Is there something in your life that could take your attention away from Jesus and become an idol?

Day 25: Eric Liddell part 3

Bible Truth: Sometimes, as we seek God's glory first, we may find ourselves standing alone for his truth.

The 1924 Olympics were being held in Paris, France. Eric had qualified to go to the Olympics and represent his home country of Scotland. He was to compete in his best event, the 100-meter dash. Eric was excited, for he once said, "When I run, I feel God's pleasure". He was the favorite to win the gold medal in this event at the Olympic games. Just before the games began, the race schedule was posted. Eric noticed that his race was scheduled to be run on a Sunday. Eric believed that Sundays were set aside for Christians to worship Christ by attending church services. Eric refused to run the race, quoting Exodus 20:8, "Remember the Sabbath day, to keep it holy".

Eric made a choice to stand for what he thought was right with God, even if it meant he would lose out on worldly success, including a gold medal. Eric wanted to honor God above his own interests. His country began to call him a traitor, or an enemy. They were angry that Eric would choose his faithfulness to God over winning for their country. Eric wanted to glorify God with his decision, regardless of the consequences. Eric wanted to show to all, what honoring Jesus looked like in his life, by choosing to do the right thing and standing alone, even if it would cost him much. Afterall, the price that Jesus paid to redeem him was a much higher cost than a gold medal.

Truth Verse(s): Matthew 6:33a and James 4:17

Day 26: Bible Discussion

Bible Truth: Sometimes, as we seek God's glory first, we may find ourselves standing alone for his truth.

Truth Verse(s): Matthew 6:33a and James 4:17

Bible Story: Read Esther 2:5-9, 3:8-10, 4:8-16

Esther became Queen in place of Vashti, who angered the king. While Esther held her position as Queen, Haman, a right-hand man to King Ahasuerus created a plan to destroy the Jews throughout the region. The King was not aware that Queen Esther was a Jew. Mordecai requested Esther to make intercession for the Jewish people to the King. However, the law said if anyone, including the Queen, came before the King in the inner court without being called, they could be killed, unless the King held out the golden sceptre. Esther was hesitant for her life though. Mordecai told Esther, what if God had put you in the kingdom as Queen, for this exact moment in time, to save your people? He said, "who knoweth whether thou are come to the kingdom for such a time as this?". Esther gave a few instructions and trusted the consequences that she would face for standing up for the Lord and his people. God gave her much grace in the sight of King Ahasuerus, that when she approached the inner court, the King gladly received her. Esther made known the evil plot of Haman and was able to have new laws written to save her people from destruction.

Thought: Has there been a time in your life when you should have spoken up or stood up for what was right, but did not because of fear of consequences?

Day 27: Eric Liddell part 4

Bible Truth: God will honor those that honor Him.

It looked as though Eric had given up his "once in a lifetime" opportunity to win a gold medal. But with God, all things are possible. A team-mate of Eric, who had already run one Olympic event, requested that Eric take his place in the 400-meter dash instead. The suggestion was brought before the Olympic Committee, and it was agreed to allow Eric to run in the 400-meter race instead of the 100-meter race. Now, Eric was the favorite to win gold in the 100-meter race, but the 400-meter run was not a race that Eric had much experience.

Just before the start of the Olympic 400-meter race, an American approached Eric on the track. He handed Eric a piece of paper. On that paper, was something that would encourage Eric as this race was about to start. It simply read, "I Samuel 2:30, 'For them that honor me, I will honor'". Eric folded up that piece of paper tightly in his hand as the runners lined up to start the race. Soon after the gunshot sounded and Eric's head was tilted back and with arms flailing, as he rounded the last leg of the race and crossed the finish line first. Eric had won the gold medal and set a new world record! God had made Eric fast, out of this world fast, and honored him by allowing him to win a gold medal that day in 1924 in a race that was new to Eric. But there was a new race that Eric would soon be starting for God, a race of far more importance.

Truth Verse(s): I Samuel 2:30 and John 12:26

Day 28: Bible Discussion

Bible Truth: God will honor those that honor Him.

Truth Verse(s): I Samuel 2:30 and John 12:26

Bible Story: Read II Chronicles 1:7-12, 9:1-8

God came to Solomon in a dream to told him to ask for anything. Instead of asking for something that would bring glory to himself or worldly treasures, Solomon asked for wisdom and knowledge to stand and rule before the people of Israel. This was something that honored God. God was very pleased with Solomon's request and as a result, God promised to honor Solomon in return. Solomon was granted great wisdom and knowledge and wealth beyond measure. There was never a king like Solomon, before or after him. The truth of how God honored and blessed Solomon spread far and wide that even when the Queen of Sheba visited, she said Solomon exceeded the fame that she had heard of abroad. Just like Solomon chose to honor God by asking for wisdom and knowledge to lead God's people, Eric pleased God by honoring the sabbath day and standing for what he thought was right. God was able to return the honor that Eric showed, by allowing him to run a different event in the Olympics, giving him the opportunity to win that gold medal and set a new world record.

Thought: Are you living to honor God in the decisions and actions that you make daily?

Day 29: Eric Liddell part 5

Bible Truth: God calls us all to a different race and each of us have different responsibilities in the work of his ministry.

Eric was walking away from his fame and success as an Olympic champion and preparing for a new race in life. God called him back to the mission field in China. His desire was to be used by God to reach the Chinese people whom he lived with as a boy. Eric encouraged himself with his favorite verse, I Corinthians 9:24, "Know ye not that they which run in a race run all, but one receiveth the prize? So, run that ye may obtain". There was a new prize that Eric had his eye on. It outweighed the gold medal by far. This was a race for souls to be saved, and a race to live his entire life for God. Eric was determined.

Eric left for China within a year after the Olympics. It was time for God to use all the talents that He had given Eric in a far greater way. Eric would share the love of Christ with the lost people in China. When Eric reached China, he began his work as a missionary teacher. God prepared Eric by studying chemistry in school and now Eric taught chemistry at the Anglo-Chinese College. Eric also assisted in building a sports complex and organized sports at the college, using more of his expertise. While Eric had an opportunity to teach young men about sports, he had an even greater opportunity to start a Bible class and a Bible study at the school. Eric led many young men to the Lord and saw forty-nine of those men baptized. Eric also preached at Union Church in Tientsin as God used him in many ways.

Truth Verse(s): Ephesians 4:11-12

Day 30: Bible Discussion

Bible Truth: God calls us all to a different race and each of us have different responsibilities in the work of his ministry.

Truth Verse(s): Ephesians 4:11-12

Bible Story: Read Acts 6:1-8

In these times, the disciples of Christ were multiplied. However, the Grecians rose with a complaint against the Christians. They said the Christians were neglecting their widows. God had called the twelve disciples to preach the word of the Lord for others to be saved, not serve in daily ministration. God calls everyone to their own duties and race. Therefore, the disciples sought out capable men, full of the Holy Ghost, faith, and wisdom, to appoint the duties of daily ministration. All jobs are equally important for the work of the Lord to move forward. Stephen was one of the men chosen since God had given him specific character qualities and prepared him to be called to this position. Just like the disciples sought out Stephen to take on some work in the ministry so the Word of God could move forward, God called Eric to use his experience with chemistry and sports at a college to open the door for the Word of God to go forth.

Thought: Is there something you have wanted to do for the Lord, but felt it either too small of a task, or that you may be too small to bring it to life? Be faithful in the little things, and God will be able to use you greatly in your race. Remember, your race will be different than others'. Do not compare your race to others. Be content with what God calls you to do.

Day 31: Eric Liddell part 6

Bible Truth: If we trust God with all our hearts, He will direct our paths.

Eric soon fell in love with a young lady named Florence. The two were married shortly after. At this time, the London Missionary Society had approached Eric about leaving the school and moving to a more rural area in China which needed more missionaries. At first, Eric did not want to leave the school. He was comfortable with teaching chemistry and being involved with the athletics of the school. However, after more prayer and consideration, Eric agreed to allow God to use him elsewhere and Eric fully surrendered to God's will for his life.

Eric trusted that God was in control of his life. If God could equip him to serve thus far on the mission field, God would certainly provide what he needed in this new area in China and ministry. Trusting the Lord, Eric left for the Siaochang Mission Complex, which is where he once lived as a child. This was a much more dangerous place than Tientsin, so Eric left his family back in Tientsin. Eric looked at this as an opportunity to bring hope to the hopeless, a smile and a laugh, and the love of God to a people who needed Jesus Christ the most.

Eric became the Pastor at a church in Siaochang. But the turn of events in China during this time, would soon bring incredibly challenging and difficult times.

Truth Verse(s): Proverbs 3:5-6 and Psalm 37:23

Day 32: Bible Discussion

Bible Truth: If we trust God with all our hearts, He will direct our paths.

Truth Verse(s): Proverbs 3:5-6 and Psalm 37:23

Bible Story: Read Exodus 3:1-2, 9-17

Moses had fled from Pharaoh in Egypt after killing an Egyptian and desiring to suffer affliction with his people, the Israelites. He made his way to Midian, where he kept the flock of Jethro and started a family. Moses spent about 40 years in Midian tending sheep and this became very familiar and comfortable to him. But one day, Moses saw the burning bush and approached it. God spoke to Moses from the burning bush and called Moses to go back to Egypt and help deliver the Israelites from being slaves to Pharaoh. Moses was very reluctant at first. He gave God quite a few excuses as to why it may not be a good idea to go back to Egypt and how he was not equipped to handle the job. But God, encouraged Moses. He reminded Moses that He is, "I AM THAT I AM" and with God, nothing is too hard or impossible with Him. Just as God worked in Moses' heart to leave what was familiar and the comfort he had come to know, God used prayer with Eric to move his heart too to advance towards the new will God had for Eric's life. Eric trusted God, even in the uncertainty, when he felt unsure and unfamiliar with what God was calling him to do.

Thought: Is God calling you out of your comfort zone to try something new for Him?

Day 33: Eric Liddell part 7

Bible Truth: Jesus Christ died for anyone who will call upon Him for salvation and is no respecter of persons.

In 1937, while Eric was pastoring in Siaochang, the Japanese invaded China and many wars and battles began to take place throughout the land. China was becoming a more dangerous and hostile place to live. Although Eric was stationed at Siaochang Mission Complex, he traveled to many of the nearby villages to share the gospel of Christ. Day in and day out, sounds of explosions and machine guns could be heard, sometimes not very far from where Eric was traveling. Many times, as he reached villages, he saw nothing but devastation of burnt homes and dead people. But Eric continued for Christ.

His brother Rob had to leave the hospital work at Siaochang which meant that Eric would now be responsible for the hospital too. Eric did not want to turn anyone away from the hospital, enemy or friend. People would often ask him why he would treat the enemy. Eric's response was, "They are neither Japanese nor Chinese, soldiers or civilians. They are all men that Christ died for". Eric understood that all men were made in the image of God and Jesus Christ died for anyone who would call upon His name for salvation.

With the war raging on, and life in China extremely dangerous, just what would Eric decide to do with his family?

Truth Verse(s): John 3:16, Romans 2:11 and Galatians 3:28-29

Day 34: Bible Discussion

Bible Truth: Jesus Christ died for anyone who will call upon Him for salvation and is no respecter of persons.

Truth Verse(s): John 3:16, Romans 2:11 and Galatians 3:28-29

Bible Story: Read Numbers 21:4-9, John 3:14-18, Roman 3:23, 6:23, 5:8, and 10:13

Jesus uses an analogy to compare himself being lifted on the cross, to that of the serpent that Moses lifted in the wilderness. God had brought a plague on the Jews in the wilderness due to sin. However, those who exercised faith could be cured and saved from the curse by looking up to the serpent that Moses had put on a pole. In the same manner, those who have faith, and by faith only believing that Jesus Christ came to die for the sins of the world and rose again the third day, can be cured from their sin sickness and have everlasting life. Jesus plainly teaches that God sent Him to this world to save the world. Jesus explains that whosoever will believe in Him and repent, will not perish but gain eternal life in heaven. The verse(s) in the book of Romans provides these truths. All, meaning everyone, have sinned. The payment for sin is death, separation from God forever in a place called hell. But God, even while we were his enemies, gave us a free gift of eternal life though his Son, Jesus Christ. God gives us salvation through forgiveness of sins when we repent, turning from our sin. God gives the power to overcome sin through the work of Jesus. And that victory is available to whosoever, meaning anyone who will call upon Jesus in truth.

Thought: Have you placed your faith and trust in Jesus Christ?

Day 35: Eric Liddell part 8

Bible Truth: We should not fear because Jesus will never leave us nor forsake us.

The war in China began to worsen with each given day. Eric had decided to send his wife and two daughters back to Canada, which was his wife's home country. He felt this was necessary for their safety. Eric decided to remain in China, expecting that within the next couple of years, he would leave for furlough to reunite with his family.

After Florence and his daughters left for Canada, Eric received a letter from Florence. She let him know that he was now the father of a new baby girl! Eric was overjoyed at the thought of his new baby girl although he had not yet met her. Little did Eric know at the time that he would never have a chance to meet his new baby.

In 1942, the Japanese requested that all foreigners to China leave the country. However, Eric refused. Eric had already established his eternal home in heaven because there was a time he had repented of his sins and asked Jesus to save him, putting his faith and trust in the finished work of Jesus Christ on the cross.

Because Eric had received the free gift of forgiveness and salvation through Jesus Christ, he was able to continue to serve the Lord without fear of what could happen to him. Eric knew his future in heaven was secure, but what about others?

Truth Verse(s): Hebrews 13:5 and Psalm 118:6

Day 36: Bible Discussion

Bible Truth: We should not fear as Jesus will never leave us nor forsake us.

Truth Verse(s): Hebrews 13:5 and Psalm 118:6

Bible Story: Judges 6:11-16

Gideon was a judge of Israel that became a mighty man of valor. But before he became a mighty man of valor, Gideon was afraid. Gideon was threshing wheat while he hid by a winepress in fear. An angel appeared to him and told him the Lord was with him. He called Gideon a mighty man of valor. Gideon was confused as Israel had been taken captive by the Midianites at this time. The Lord spoke to Gideon and told him to be mighty as the Lord had called Gideon to deliver Israel from the hand of the Midianites. Gideon of course was afraid to rise and lead Israel in battle. He gave the Lord a few different excuses as to why God had the wrong guy for the job. But the Lord promised Gideon that He would go with him and that He would indeed defeat the Midianites.

Just as Gideon was afraid of the uncertainty, he chose to place his trust in the Lord, because the Lord would be with him. Eric did the same as he refused to leave China and stay to serve Jesus, not knowing what the future would behold. Both Gideon and Eric trusted the promise of the Lord to go with them into difficult circumstances.

Thought: Is there something you fear? Remember, greater is He that is in you than he that is in the world.

Day 37: Eric Liddell part 9

Bible Truth: God wants us to be joyful and help others, even in difficult times.

Eric, as well as other missionaries and foreigners who refused to leave China, were required by the Japanese to report to prisons. Eric boarded a train to the prison camp in Weihsien. As he settled on the train, he looked to God's word for encouragement. Eric knew this was going to be a difficult time. But Eric was determined to finish the race that God had given him with a good attitude and a cheerful heart.

There were over 1800 prisoners in the camp at Weihsien. Eric determined in his heart to serve the Lord and help make this prison camp a better place to live.

Many people at the camp recognized Eric as an Olympic gold medal champion. He was the celebrity of the camp amongst the teenagers and kids who were naturally drawn to him. He organized sports activities, taught science classes, and helped with everyday mundane jobs such as fetching water, taking out trash, and gathering coal at the prison camp. Eric started a Bible study and saw many people saved. Eric took on a new role of Christian counselor.

Eric was an inspiration to others and showed joy while serving the Lord and others in this difficult time. He strived to love and put others first. People would soon see just how much Eric loved others above himself.

Truth Verse(s): Nehemiah 8:10b and I Thessalonians 5:16-18

Day 38: Bible Discussion

Bible Truth: God wants us to be joyful and help others, even in difficult times.

Truth Verse(s): Nehemiah 8:10b and I Thessalonians 5:16-18

Bible Story: Acts 16:22-34

Paul and Silas had just been beaten and thrown into the inner prison. They did not let their circumstances bring them down though. At midnight, Paul and Silas prayed and sang praises to the Lord for all the prisoners to hear. Suddenly, a great earthquake shook the prison and unlocked all the doors and chains on the prisoners. They were free! But rather than flee, Paul and Silas remained in jail. The guard of the jail awoke and saw the prison doors open. He pulled out a sword to take his life for losing the prisoners, but Paul cried out to the guard to put his sword down and not harm himself. The keeper of the prison took Paul and Silas back to his house and listened as they shared the gospel and how to be saved with the guard. The prison guard got saved and helped clean and bandage the wounds of Paul and Silas.

Even amid the difficult trials and circumstances that Paul and Silas found themselves in, they still managed to have joy and serve the Lord. This is exactly what Eric did as he ministered to others in the prison camp, using all his talents, gifts, and experiences to reach others with the gospel.

Thought: Are there situations you find yourself in that you may not feel like being joyful?

Day 39: Eric Liddell part 10

Bible Truth: God will give grace to run your race and will reward his servants for their job well done.

Eric knew every day was a gift from God, even in hard times. Eric always chose to put God and others first. This could not be more evident in what would happen next.

Winston Churchill was able to arrange a prisoner exchange and Eric was going to be freed. Eric would return to his family in Canada and meet his newest daughter. However, Eric put others first. He allowed a pregnant lady prisoner to take his place in the prisoner exchange rather than himself. She was able to go free while he remained in the prison camp.

Eric soon became terribly ill while in the camp. He had a brain tumor that was not able to be treated medically. Eric died shortly after in the prison camp. He never reunited with his family. He never met his youngest daughter. But Eric lived a life summed up by the words he once spoke, "It has been a wonderful experience to compete in the Olympic Games and to bring home a gold medal. But since I have been a young lad, I have had my eyes on a different prize. You see, each one of us is in a greater race than any I have run in Paris, and this race ends when God gives out the medals".

Eric was called home and surely heard, "well done my good and faithful servant". He lived a life surrendered to God and others, even in the most challenging times.

Truth Verse(s): I Corinthians 3:13-14 and Revelation 2:10

Day 40: Bible Discussion

Bible Truth: God will give grace to run your race and will reward his servants for their job well done.

Truth Verse(s): I Corinthians 3:13-14 and Revelation 2:10

Bible Story: II Timothy 2:1-5 and II Timothy 4:5-8

This letter was the second letter written by Paul to young Timothy, the Pastor of the church at Ephesus. This letter was written near the end of Paul's ministry. Paul encourages Timothy to endure difficult and hard times as a good soldier of Jesus Christ. This reminds us that we are indeed soldiers on God's side in the spiritual battle every day. We are going to face hardships. Paul states that we should not war with the affairs of the world, but in the spiritual battle. As soldiers of Christ and in the race that God has called us to, we should strive for mastery. In a race, you only win the prize, crown, or medal, if you do so by the rules and finish. Paul writes how he had fought the good fight of Jesus Christ and kept the faith to the end. Paul knows there is a crown and rewards that await him from the Lord for he completed his race with faith to the end. Paul reminds us that each one of us will receive a crown and reward if we strive to run our race in a way that is pleasing to the Lord.

Eric certainly ran his race to please the Lord. Eric fought the good fight. Eric kept the faith, just as Paul did. Eric will receive his rewards in heaven from the Lord Jesus, just like Paul.

Thought: Are you striving in your race to please the Lord?

Solomon Ginsberg

Missionary to Brazil

Day 41: Solomon Ginsburg part 1

Bible Truth: Ask questions, seek God, and knock on his door. He will answer.

Solomon Ginsburg was about thirteen. Solomon did not know Jesus Christ as the Messiah or his Savior, but God was getting ready to intervene.

Solomon was a Jewish boy. His father was a Jewish Rabbi hosting a group of men as they celebrated the Feast of the Tabernacles. His father decided that since Solomon was thirteen, he could keep company with the men. Under the tent where the men celebrated, was a table piled with books. Solomon picked up a very worn copy of the book of prophets. He unintentionally flipped the book to Isaiah chapter 53.

As Solomon read the chapter silently, he noticed a note scribbled in the side margin. The note read, "Who does the prophet speak of"? Solomon began to wonder the same thing. In front of the men, Solomon asked his father who the prophet was referring to? His father ignored him, and so Solomon innocently asked him again. At that moment, Solomon's father grabbed the book from Solomon's hand and slapped him across his face in front of all the men. Solomon was very hurt and embarrassed and yet his question was not answered that day. But God was preparing the perfect opportunity to answer Solomon's question, which would be made clear within the next couple of years of young Solomon's life.

Truth Verse(s): Deuteronomy 4:9 and Matthew 7:7

Day 42: Bible Discussion

Bible Truth: Ask questions, seek God, and knock on his door. He will answer.

Truth Verse(s): Deuteronomy 4:9 and Matthew 7:7

Bible Lesson: Acts 8:26-38

An Ethiopian eunuch was traveling home by chariot, reading the book of Isaiah. God knew the Ethiopian was seeking to know who God was. God sent his servant Philip to catch up to the chariot. As Philip joined himself to the chariot, he heard the Ethiopian reading the book of Isaiah. Philip asked him if he understood what he was reading. The Ethiopian responded that he did not understand and needed someone to explain it to him. He asked Philip to join him in the chariot and help him with the portion of scripture. Philip began to speak of Jesus Christ and how the book of Isaiah was speaking directly about gospel. Philip walked the Ethiopian through the death, burial, and resurrection of Jesus Christ, and how that Jesus Christ died to make men whole. The eunuch then asked if he could be baptized. Philip responded that if he believed on what the Lord Jesus Christ did, with all his heart, then he could indeed be baptized. The chariot stopped and the eunuch was baptized.

Just as God used Philip to help reveal himself to the Ethiopian eunuch, God would use embarrassing and hurtful memory in Solomon's life to help open his eyes to the truth.

Thought: Is there something in the Bible you do not understand? Ask, seek, and knock.

Day 43: Solomon Ginsburg part 2

Bible Truth: Jesus Christ took the punishment for our sins so if we believe and repent, we can be forgiven.

Some time had passed, and Solomon left his parent's home to live with his Jewish uncle. As he walked home one Sabbath afternoon, a Jewish missionary approached Solomon. He told Solomon he was preaching nearby that afternoon and invited Solomon along to listen. At first, Solomon was not very interested. Then the missionary told Solomon he was preaching on the 53rd chapter of Isaiah. Suddenly, Solomon's mind slipped back to when he was thirteen and his father humiliated him in front of the group of men for asking a question about this chapter; a question that had yet to be answered. Solomon decided to go to the meeting in hopes of getting a better explanation about who the prophet spoke of in Isaiah 53 than his father gave him years prior. It was at this meeting that Solomon came to know Jesus Christ as the long-awaited Jewish Messiah. Solomon's eyes were opened to see Jesus for the first time, as the Savior of the world, forgiver of sins and transgressions, and worthy of all praise.

Over the next couple of months, Solomon gave his life to Jesus Christ, to live for and to serve Christ, no matter the cost.   And you can be sure, there was going to be a cost for choosing to follow Jesus Christ.

Truth Verse(s): I John 3:5 and II Corinthians 5:21

Day 44: Bible Discussion

Bible Truth: Jesus Christ took the punishment for our sins so if we believe and repent, we can be forgiven.

Truth Verse(s): I John 3:5 and II Corinthians 5:21

Bible Lesson: Read Isaiah 53:1-12

The prophet Isaiah prophesied in this chapter of the coming Messiah, Jesus Christ. Isaiah gave very distinct and specific details about Christ's characteristics and humble life. He said there is no beauty in Christ, and we would not desire Him. Jesus's own people rejected Him. Isaiah said that Christ would be despised and rejected and know grief. The Jewish leaders and elders hated Jesus and sought to kill Him. The prophet goes on to further prophesy how Jesus would be wounded for our transgressions and bruised for our iniquities and not his. All our iniquity and sin would be laid on Jesus who was perfect without sin. Isaiah says that through the stripes of Jesus we are healed. The prophet even tells of how Jesus would go to be crucified without fighting back and be silent, like a sheep to a slaughter. The death and burial of Jesus is foretold in that He was crucified with the wicked and buried with the rich. Jesus was an offering for the world's sin. Through the suffering of Jesus, the wrath of God for sin is satisfied and many who believe shall be justified.

Solomon's eyes were opened to the truth about who Jesus was for the first time in his life.

Thought: Do you see Jesus in this prophesy? Have you given your life over to Him fully in return for what He has done for you?

Day 45: Solomon Ginsburg part 3

Bible Truth: When we stand for Jesus and truth, we will face persecution and stand alone. But God is with us.

Solomon faced great persecution as a follower of Jesus Christ. But Solomon was in good company, as Jesus faced persecution too. Solomon was kicked out of his home for believing in Jesus. As Solomon would try and tell other Jews about Jesus Christ the Messiah, he would often be severely beaten. Once, he was beaten and left for dead in a garbage bin. On another occasion, as Solomon tried to share the truth of Christ, a group attacked him with hammers and dropped him down a five-story spiral staircase.

Solomon chose to have faith over fear and follow God, who has power over eternal life. Solomon trusted God for his eternal life in heaven, and therefore, he did not fear what man could do to him. God would never forsake him. Solomon understood that if someone wanted to kill him for sharing Jesus would only result in his home going to heaven to meet his Savior. Solomon knew that not everyone would go to heaven. Only those who were drawn by the Father to a regenerate and repentant heart, who believed in who Jesus was and his atoning work on the cross, would call upon Jesus to forgive and save, would have eternal life in heaven. Solomon wanted others to know about the love of Jesus and how they could be saved. Solomon responded to God's call to be a missionary to Brazil and embarked on a new journey in serving Christ.

Truth Verse(s): John 15:20, John 16:33, and Hebrews 13:5

Day 46: Bible Discussion

Bible Truth: Sometimes, when we stand for Jesus and truth, we will face persecution and stand alone. But God is with us.

Truth Verse(s): John 15:20, John 16:33, and Hebrews 13:5

Bible Story: Matthew 14:3-12

John the Baptist was known to be the greatest born among women. John the Baptist was the one that prepared the way of the Lord. John was thrown in prison by King Herod because John stood for truth. John told King Herod that something he did was wrong. King Herod took his brother Philip's wife, Herodias, which was adultery. John told Herod he had sinned. Herodias's daughter entertained King Herod and his guests at a birthday. Pleased with the daughter, King Herod offered her anything up to half the kingdom. Herodias, her mother, told her daughter to ask for the head of John the Baptist on a charger. And so, Herod, to keep his word in front of his party, sent men to behead John while in prison and present his head in a charger to Herodias and her daughter.

John's death seemed unfair. Afterall, he was only standing for truth. The same was true for Solomon. He did not deserve to be beaten and treated with such persecution. Solomon, just like John, was only trying to share truth and help people come to repentance and know Jesus. But Jesus Himself said, all that will live godly in Christ Jesus, will face persecution.

Thought: Are you facing persecution because you are standing up for truth and what is right? You are in good company.

Day 47: Solomon Ginsburg part 4

Bible Truth: The preaching of God's Word on soft hearts leads to repentance and faith in Jesus.

Solomon soon became known in Brazil as the "Wandering Jew". He traveled to many places, sharing the good news of Jesus Christ. In each new place, Solomon would hold open air meetings. He would pull a chair in the middle of a town square, sing hymns, and then preach on the forgiveness of sins through the work of Jesus Christ on the cross. One day, as he preached an open-air message, God sent a man with a soft heart who listened intently. His message that day was titled, "The Blood of Jesus, The Son of God, Cleansing from All Sin". Maybe his message went something like this....

Romans 3:23 says all have sinned. All includes me. You. Everyone. Romans 6:23 says the punishment for sin is death in hell but the gift of God is eternal life through Jesus. You can't earn a gift, it's free. Jesus is the gift, fully God and fully man. Jesus knew no sin but became sin for us, to take our place and our punishment for our sin, not His. Romans 5:8 says that God loved us so much, He died in our place even while we were yet sinners. No greater love is this than a man would give his life for a friend. Romans 10:13 says whosoever calls upon the name of the Lord shall be saved. Today, are you a whosoever? Do you feel His call upon your heart? Call upon Him and give Him your sin in exchange for His forgiveness, His righteousness, *and His promise of eternal life.*

Truth Verse(s): Romans 10:17 and II Corinthians 5:21

Day 48: Bible Discussion

Bible Truth: The preaching of God's Word on soft hearts leads to repentance and faith in Jesus.

Truth Verse(s): Romans 10:17 and II Corinthians 5:21

Bible Story: Matthew 13:1-9

Jesus told the parable of the sower. The sower is the one who brings the word of God to people, just like Solomon was doing in Brazil. The different soils in the parable represent our heart's receptiveness and responsiveness to God's word being preached. God's word falls on deaf ears for those with hard hearts. They may believe in who Jesus is but are not willing to repent and give up their sins. James 2:19 says the devils believe and tremble. Unfortunately, not everyone who hears the word of God will be saved. Sometimes, we receive the word of God gladly, but it has not taken deep root. When trials come, a person turns away from God. In other instances, the word of God is choked out by the cares of this world. These first few soils represent a stony heart not ready to live a surrendered life to Jesus Christ. However, a seed planted today can grow into faith tomorrow. Then there is good soil, soft and ready for the planting of God's word. The Word of God takes root and changes lives. John 6:44 and 6:65 say that God the Father must draw men to Jesus. That drawing from the Father is ready soil, or soft hearts for the planting of the gospel of Jesus. Solomon preached to many people that day in his open-air meeting. That one sinner in attendance had been drawn by God with a soft heart, ready to repent and receive a new life!

Thought: Is your heart soft for what God is trying to teach you?

Day 49: Solomon Ginsburg part 5

Bible Truth: Those who repent and are truly saved are new creatures in Christ.

In the crowd that day, Herculano stood, with a soft heart, listening to every word that Solomon preached in the open-air meeting. God had prepared Herculano's heart for the truth and God was doing a work that only He could do. Solomon was able to speak with Herculano after the meeting. Herculano desired to know more of Jesus. He asked Solomon to come to his home and tell him more of God's truth, love, and forgiveness. Solomon agreed and set up a meeting for the following day.

It was known that Herculano lived in one of the worst and most dangerous areas, filled with murderers and thieves. But that did not stop Solomon from going to tell him about Jesus. Solomon was already saved and had his home in heaven. He wanted to use every opportunity to share that good news with others, even if it meant it could cost him his life. After all, Jesus had willingly given up His life for Solomon and it was the least Solomon could do to serve such a great Savior.

The next day, Solomon went to meet Herculano in his home and share the love of Jesus with him. Herculano received the word with such joy. He fell to the floor and admitted he was a sinner, pleading with Jesus to save him that day. That day, all Herculano's sins were forgiven, his name was written in the Lamb's Book of Life, and he became a new man in Christ.

Truth Verse(s): II Corinthians 5:17 and Ephesians 4:24

Day 50: Bible Discussion

Bible Truth: Those who repent and are truly saved are new creatures in Christ.

Truth Verse(s): II Corinthians 5:17 and Ephesians 4:24

Bible Lesson: Mark 5:1-15

Jesus traveled to the country of the Gadarenes. Once he made it to land, he was met by a person who was an outcast of the country. This man had evil spirits that lived in him. The man was unsafe to live with other people and therefore he lived alone in the tombs, ruled by evil spirits that indwelled him. These evil spirits would cause him harm day after day. The people tried to bind the man with chains and fetters, but he would pluck them asunder. Jesus approached the man and had a conversation with the demons that possessed him. They said their name was legion because there were many. But Jesus has all authority of everything. Jesus cast out those demons and sent them into a herd of swine on a hill. The man was immediately changed to a calm, clothed person, in his right mind. Jesus made this man a new creature.

Just like Jesus changed the man in the tombs at the Gadarenes, Jesus changed Herculano. He saved him and created in him a clean heart unto repentance. It only takes one touch from Jesus to make us whole and new.

Thought: Is there something you are trying to overcome and have not been able to? Give it to Jesus and trust Him to help you become new.

Day 51: Solomon Ginsburg part 6

Bible Truth: God gives us power to overcome sin.

Herculano told Solomon of his miserable and wicked life before he came to know Christ as his Savior. Herculano was a hired assassin for a high ranked political figure in Brazil. The politician would send Herculano out to kill people and Herculano would follow through on the hit request for money.

Herculano had just been released from prison and completed his most recent hit job a mere couple of days before hearing Solomon preach in the open-air meeting. He was so convicted by the preaching of God's Word and was ready to forsake his old life for a renewed and forgiven life with Jesus Christ. Herculano walked away from his sinful and wicked past life, the old man, in exchange for a life lived for Christ, the new man. Jesus has resurrection power to bring a dead life alive unto God.

As Solomon went on sharing the gospel and truth of Jesus Christ in Brazil, he made some religious leaders very angry. These religious leaders wanted to have Solomon killed. But the hand of God was on Solomon and God was still using him greatly to reach souls for Christ in Brazil. It turns out, Herculano would not be the only assassin that Solomon leads to Christ. But just how would God use him again, to set yet another murder free?

Truth Verse(s): John 5:14b and Romans 6:14

Day 52: Bible Discussion

Bible Truth: God gives us power to overcome sin.

Truth Verse(s): John 5:14b and Romans 6:14

Bible Lesson: John 8:1-11

Jesus had just come into the temple to teach the people. The scribes and Pharisees brought a woman into the midst of the crowd at the temple. The woman was caught in the act of adultery. The penalty for adultery was to be stoned to death. As the leaders sought Jesus to condemn the woman to death, Jesus knelt and wrote in the sand. Jesus then arose and said unto the scribes and Pharisees, you without sin, cast the first stone. Slowly, one by one, the leaders turned and left the temple. They were convicted of their own sin and conscience. In the end, the woman stood before Jesus with no accusers left. Jesus asked where are those that condemned her to death, are there none? She said none. Jesus replied that He would not condemn her either. By not condemning her, Jesus forgave her sins. Then He spoke to the woman and told her to go and sin no more. She had a new life, not the same old life, as she lived out the forgiveness Christ showed her and sinned no more.

This is the same experience that Herculano had after being saved by Jesus Christ. Just like the woman in the story, he was going to move on and sin no more.

Thought: Is there sin in your life that you struggle to overcome? Keep seeking God. He gives you the power to overcome.

Day 53: Solomon Ginsburg part 7

Bible Truth: God will accomplish his will and plan in our lives.

Solomon was warned that there was a hit put on his life by the religious group that he had angered. Solomon was told that the next time he preached, there would be an assassin in the crowd, hired to take Solomon's life. But God was not yet done with Solomon and God had plans to use Solomon more. When God is for us, nothing can stand against us. Nothing and no one can separate us from the love of God or take the eternal life from God's adopted children. Solmon moved on that day without fear, knowing his eternal destiny was sealed and God was on his side.

There was indeed a hired assassin in the crowd that day. But God intervened and fought to protect Solomon while he preached. The assassin fell asleep during the preaching and missed his opportunity to kill Solomon. Later, the assassin came to Solomon to learn about salvation through Jesus Christ, and he too became a Christian.

God was good to Solomon, protecting him throughout his time in Brazil. Solomon's faithful service to Christ brought many souls to the foot of the cross for salvation and the gospel seed planted throughout the country. Through Solomon's trust and courage in the Lord, assassins were converted, churches were started, and prisoners throughout Brazil received printed copies of the New Testament Bible and Christian literature!

Truth Verse(s): I Samuel 12:24 and I Corinthians 15:58

Day 54: Bible Discussion

Bible Truth: God will accomplish his will and plan in our lives.

Truth Verse(s): I Samuel 12:24 and I Corinthians 15:58

Bible Story: Acts 23:11, Acts 25:10-12, Acts 27:1,22-26, 42-44, & Acts 28:3-6, 16

While Paul was in prison at Jerusalem, God spoke to Paul in a vision that Paul would go to Rome to testify of Jesus. But Rome was far away, and Paul was in prison. God began to make things happen in Paul's life to carry out His will for Paul. Paul testified of Jesus in the prison and after a plot arose to kill him, Paul was taken to Caesarea. Paul was tried before Felix and then Festus. They found no fault in Paul and may have freed him; however, Paul had appealed to go before Cesar to Rome. After Paul spoke with King Agrippa, he was put on a ship headed to Rome. After a ship change, a great storm arose. The prisoners, guards, and crew members were shipwrecked. But Paul remembered and trusted the promise of God that he was going to Rome. He told the others that no one would die, and they would be safe on an island for a short time. After surviving the ocean, Paul gathered firewood with the tribal people of the island when a viper bit him. The natives waited for Paul to swell up and die, but nothing happened. After a season on the island, Paul and the gang sailed off again and finally made it to Rome.

Just like God had a plan for Paul, God had a plan for Solomon. And God would not allow harm to happen to Solomon until his will, purpose, and mission was complete.

Thought: Are you seeking the Lord's plan for your life?

Henry Nott

Missionary to Tahiti

Day 55: Henry Nott part 1

Bible Truth: God prepares us for his work and guides our paths.

The year was 1774. In a town called Bromsgrove, England, a young man was born that would have a great eternal impact on an entire nation, including kings. That young man was Henry Nott.

As Henry grew up, he became a brick layer. Being a brick layer was very hard work. It was dirty and required long, hot hours in the summer sun. But being a brick layer was only temporary. Although Henry did not know it yet, God had a very different plan for his life. Many times, as God directs our path according to his will, he will prepare us for that task through current events, situations, and people in our life. And that is just what God was doing to prepare Henry for what lay ahead.

God led Henry to join the London Missionary Society. In September of 1796, Henry boarded "The Duff" and sailed to a group of islands known as The Society Islands.

The trip overseas would be a long and tiring journey. Finally, after 6 months of sailing, Henry Nott, and a few other missionary friends, made landfall on the island of Tahiti.

Henry never guessed that this would be his home for the next 50 years. God would use Henry here to minister to lost souls, share the gospel, and reach even royalty with the love of Jesus.

Truth Verse(s): Jeremiah 29:11 and Ephesians 2:10

Day 56: Bible Discussion

Bible Truth: God prepares us for his work and guides our paths.

Truth Verse(s): Jeremiah 29:11 and Ephesians 2:10

Bible Story: Acts 9:1-16

Saul was a Pharisee. He brought great persecution to the church. Saul was very well educated and learned in all the Jewish customs and religion practices. As Saul was on his way to Damascus, a bright light shone round about. Saul fell to the earth and Jesus began to speak to Saul. Jesus asked Saul, "why persecutest thou me"? Saul was blinded and Jesus gave him instructions to go into the city and wait. Jesus then told Ananias to go to Saul and put his hands on him so he would receive his sight. Jesus said that Saul is a chosen vessel to be used by Him and how Saul would suffer great things for the name of Christ.

Paul, formerly Saul, understood about persecution of the church very clearly. Paul would suffer great things for Christ. God would also use Paul's childhood education and religious training of the Jewish law. God had prepared Paul, even at a young age, for the work of the ministry. Paul grew up under the Old Testament law and had a very clear understanding of the coming Messiah. God would use this knowledge that Paul learned as a child to point people to the Messiah through fulfilled prophesy, making a distinction between the old covenant (the law) and the new covenant only found in Christ.

Just as God worked in Paul and Henry's life at an early age, God is working in your life to prepare you for his will.

Thought: What could God use in your life now, for later?

Day 57: Henry Nott part 2

Bible Truth: It's vain to gain the whole world and lose your soul.

When Henry arrived on the Island of Tahiti, there was a king over the tribes of the land whose name was King Otu. He was very young and had only the title of king. It was really his father, King Pomare, who made the decisions. King Pomare had very wicked practices, including the sacrifice of humans. It was said during King Pomare's reign, he had sacrificed over 2000 people to his false gods. This struck fear into the lives of many, but not Henry, who had someone much more powerful on his side.

On the contrary, King Pomare was quite friendly with Henry and the missionaries. Henry found the custom of the king and queen being carried on the shoulders of their servants everywhere to be strange. King Pomare was carried many times to share feasts with Henry. One day, the servants not only carried the king, but also a large trunk. When Henry asked what the trunk was for, King Pomare responded, "to carry the gifts you will be pleased to give me". Henry gave him all that he requested: axes, shirts, mirrors, scissors, nails, combs, razors, and blankets. The King was not concerned about the true gift that Henry had to share, only treasures he could see and touch. Henry shared the gospel with King Pomare for 6 years. But the king never accepted the true treasure of eternal life through Christ. He died, unforgiven, in his sins, in 1803, and went to his eternal home in hell.

Truth Verse(s): Matthew 6:33 and Matthew 6:21

Day 58: Bible Discussion

Bible Truth: It's vain to gain the whole world and lose your soul.

Truth Verse(s): Matthew 6:33 and Matthew 6:21

Bible Story: Luke 16:19-25

The rich man in the parable lived life very comfortably. He had fine clothes to wear. He had the best food that money could buy. The rich man lacked nothing physically. His heart's desire was for tangible goods. He did not care about other people or their needs. The rich man did not care about things of heaven above, his soul being saved, God, or where he would spend eternity. All that mattered to him was the treasures he could have today in things he could see and hold. One day, both Lazarus the poor man and the rich man died. Lazarus, who was poor on earth and did not even have so much as food to eat, went to live in heaven with Jesus. The rich man, who only cared about himself and his goods on earth, went to eternity in hell.

Just like the rich man in the parable, King Pomare was only concerned about goods and riches on earth. He had no desire of heavenly things, God, or his soul's salvation and eternal home. It is vanity if you gain the entire world and its riches but lose your soul for eternity. This lifetime is only a small part compared to where you will spend your eternal life. Once you die, you do not get a second chance to change your soul's eternal destination. That must be decided by you ahead of time.

Thought: Do you find yourself focusing more on what the world has to offer, or those things concerning heaven above?

Day 59: Henry Nott part 3

Bible Truth: Wait on and trust God. He will never leave you. He will be your strength.

Henry was sad that after 6 years of sharing Jesus with King Pomare, he didn't trust Christ for salvation. This was just the beginning of challenges that Henry would face in Tahiti.

Thievery was common in Tahiti. Almost two-thirds of babies born were sacrificed to false gods. The sick and old were buried alive without thought for their lives. The sinful wickedness in Tahiti was unspeakable. It was a dark place to live.

As the missionary's gifts to the tribe ran low, they were robbed of almost everything they had, including those things they needed to survive. Henry and the missionaries went their first four years without replenishment of supplies and would only receive two shipments over the next seven years. Their clothes were tattered and thread bare. They often scoured the mountains for wild fruit to eat. Their homes were destroyed. Their printing press was melted down to make bullets. Their lives had become endangered. After thirteen years of serving with other missionaries in Tahiti, the other missionaries abandoned Henry and he found himself alone.

Henry did not give up though. Henry trusted that God would never leave him nor forsake him and strengthened himself in the Lord.

Truth Verse(s): Isaiah 40:31 and Hebrews 13:5

Day 60: Bible Discussion

Bible Truth: Wait on and trust God. He will never leave you. He will be your strength.

Truth Verse(s): Isaiah 40:31 and Hebrews 13:5

Bible Story: Job 1:8-22, Job 2:3-10, Job 42:12

Job was a believer and a follower of God. One day, when the angels were presenting themselves before God, Satan did too. God asked Satan if he considered his servant Job. Satan replied that Job only serves God faithfully because God had blessed him with so much. God agreed to allow Satan to put his hand against him and take away everything he had. Satan had Job robbed of his oxen, asses, and camels and burned his sheep. Satan had Job's servants killed as well as all ten of his children. But Job did not sin or turn from following God. God than granted Satan the opportunity to take away Job's health. Satan struck him with boils from head to toe. Job's wife told him that he should curse God and die. Job did not sin against God. He remained faithful to God and understood that God can give and take away, yet God is still God. Job remained patient and faithful to follow God. God blessed Job greater in the later end than in his beginning.

Just as Job faced difficult trials, Henry had his share too. But neither of them turned away from God. They trusted God. God would bless them richly in the end for their faithfulness through difficult times.

Thought: What trials or difficulties are you going through that cause you to doubt God? Remember, God is always good!

Day 61: Henry Nott part 4

Bible Truth: God makes us new creatures in Christ and gives us new desires.

Henry continued to serve Jesus in Tahiti as well as the neighboring islands. He had such a desire to share the gospel and preached John 3:16 time and again to the natives. Since the death of King Pomare, Henry gave special attention to his son, King Otu, also known as King Pomare II.

Henry shared the gospel for sixteen years in Tahiti. Finally, after all those years of labor, King Otu's heart was responding to the gospel. Henry was finally going to see his first fruits in Tahiti!

King Otu called upon Jesus to save his life! He became a new man, a new creature, a new king. He destroyed the idols that he found across the land. He set up schools for children to learn. King Otu took the lead on heathen practices being abandoned. The gospel had changed not only for King Otu, but many across the island as well.

Thousands of natives came to hear Henry preach and many became Christians. The island became more civilized. With the help of Henry, King Otu posted a new set of laws for his people to follow. Powerful changes took place because of Christ.

These were joyous moments for Henry in his missionary work in Tahiti. Yet there was something great that was still to come.

Truth verse(s): II Corinthians 5:17 and Ephesians 4:22-24

Day 62: Bible Discussion

Bible Truth: God makes us new creatures in Christ and gives us new desires.

Truth Verse(s): II Corinthians 5:17 and Ephesians 4:22-24

Bible Story: Luke 8:1-3, John 19:25, John 20:11-16

Mary Magdelene had been overcome with evil. We can just imagine what evil Mary was involved with when she had 7 devils living in her. She was a puppet to the evil one and a slave to sin and destruction. She was a threat, not only to herself, but to all those around her. Yet Jesus had compassion on Mary and cast out those 7 devils. Immediately, Mary became a new creature with new desires, to follow Christ. Mary traveled along with Jesus as He went about from town to town. She also used her finances and substance to minister to Jesus. She had a new desire to love Jesus and the things that Jesus loved. She forsook her old ways and fully decided to follow Him. Mary was faithful to Christ after He saved her. She was seen at the foot of the cross when He died. And better yet, Mary was there to minister to Jesus even after his death. Mary was the first person that Jesus spoke to after his resurrection.

Mary became a new creature in Christ just like King Otu. Their old nature was changed from darkness to light, and both were given new desires to serve and whole heartedly follow Christ.

Thought: Are you all in to serve and follow God? Are there areas in your life that you still need to give to God so He can cultivate more Christ-like desires and attitudes?

Day 63: Henry Nott part 5

Bible Truth: We are all called to the great commission!

Henry Knott had finally seen his first convert after 16 years of serving in Tahiti. And it was quite a convert, the king himself! King Otu wasted no time growing in grace and helping the gospel and the love of Christ reach the natives of his country.

In 1819, the King provided materials to build a church at Papaoa. The church was so big it had three pulpits that could be used at the same time without interruption. The church was called, 'The Royal Mission'. It was dedicated on May 11, 1819. Twenty-two years after arriving in Tahiti as a missionary, Henry saw his first convert baptized, King Pomare II. There were over 5,000 people at the baptism for the king.

The harvest in Tahiti was ready. New missionaries, as well as some of Henry's old co-laborers had come to Tahiti to help. Over the next ten years, several hundred natives had become Christians and were eagerly studying God's Word. Some even focused on winning souls on the nearby islands.

Henry preached and ministered in Tahiti for nearly fifty years. By 1838, he completed printing the New Testament in the Tahitian language. His favorite verse to preach was John 3:16, which Henry read to Queen Elizabeth back in England from a newly printed Tahitian Bible. Henry served God in Tahiti for fifty years, until God called him home on May 1, 1844, at the age of seventy. Only heaven knows the full impact of Henry's work!

Truth Verse(s): Matthew 28:18-20 and Luke 24:47

Day 64: Bible Discussion

Bible Truth: We are all called to the great commission!

Truth Verse(s): Matthew 28:18-20 and Luke 24:47

Bible Story: Romans 10:11-17 and Titus 1:2-3

In this portion of scripture, Paul is speaking truth on how a person can be saved. Paul makes it very clear that there is no difference between the Jew or the Greek when it comes to salvation. Salvation through faith in Christ is for all people. Paul states to be saved, you must call upon the name of the Lord. But then Paul poses the questions…how can they be saved if they have not believed? How can they believe if they have not heard? How can they hear without a preacher? How shall they preach except they be sent forth? Those who take the gospel to others have a beautiful message to share. Paul then shares with Titus, that although in times past God had spoken through prophets, tongues, and great wonders, in current times, eternal life is manifested through His Word, the Bible, being preached.

Just as Paul went about preaching and sharing the Word of God, Henry did as well. King Otu even had a part in the Word being preached when he supplied the materials to build a church and pulpit for the Word to go forth. Faith comes by hearing the Word of God. Paul understood this and so did Henry and King Otu. We, as Christians, have an obligation to be a part of getting the Word of God out to unbelievers too.

Thought: What activities or events can you be involved with to help get the gospel out to those who have not heard?

David Brainerd

Missionary to Indians in New Jersey and Delaware

Day 65: David Brainerd part 1

Bible Truth: God protects and fights for his children.

The sun had set as the glow of the fire flickered in the night. A frail, sickly young man, on bended knee, was in his tent, in deep fervent prayer. The stars popped out in the night, making the night seem to the young man praying, all was calm. Oh, but little did he know the danger that awaited, both inside and outside of his tent that night.

His tent camp was surrounded by savage Indians who waited for just the right moment to attack and kill the pale faced white man. They watched and they waited intently for just the right moment to surprise their victim and bring his life to an end.

Little did the Indians know though, that the young man had someone far greater working on his behalf. While the young man was deep in prayer, God was already working on his behalf to protect him. God would use this dangerous situation to not only shine forth his glory and power, but to also open the door for this young man to be able to share Christ with the savage Indians.

But just who was this young man on bended knee, deep in prayer to God in heaven? His name is David Brainerd.

Truth Verse(s): Deuteronomy 20:4 and Exodus 14:14

Day 66: Bible Discussion

Bible Truth: God protects and fights for his children.

Truth Verse(s): Deuteronomy 20:4 and Exodus 14:14

Bible Story: II Kings 6:8-18

The king of Syria had war with Israel and told his servants where to set his camp for an ambush against Israel. God sent a message unto Elisha to warn the king of Israel not to pass by that place. The king of Syria was mad and thought that one of his men betrayed him, warning the king of Israel not to pass that way. But his men told him it was the man of God that warned the king of Israel. The king of Syria was wroth and sent a great host with horses and chariots to capture Elisha. When the servant of Elisha went outside, he saw the great host of the king of Syria and was afraid. Elisha told him to fear not, for the army on their side was far greater than those of the king of Syria. Elisha prayed for God to open his servant's eyes so he could see the horses and chariots of fire that God had sent to protect them and fight for them.

Just like God sent his army to protect Elisha and his servant, God was fighting for David while he prayed in his tent. And just as Elisha's servant's eyes were not opened to see God's army, David's eyes were blind to the battle that God was fighting for him too.

Thought: Are you trusting the Lord to fight for you and not taking matters into your own hands?

Day 67: David Brainerd part 2

Bible Truth: God uses the weak to reflect his power and strength.

David Brainerd was born in 1718 in Haddam, Connecticut. David, although very weak, would become a man greatly used by God.

David's battles and difficulties were great. From the very beginning of life, he faced many challenges. He had a melancholy spirit that drew him into depression, especially after the death of his parents by the age of fourteen. He would endure setbacks at college too. Even greater than these was David's poor health. David had a disease called tuberculosis and would die at the young age of 29. David's struggles with tuberculosis would plague him on the mission field. The place he called home, a tent in the woods, in the open brutality of the seasons and inclement weather, would further complicate his disease.

Despite David's weaknesses, God called him to be a missionary. to the savage Indians in the providences of Delaware and New Jersey. David was a missionary in the 1700's but his ministry still lives on today, as an inspiration and encouragement to thousands of Christians through the work of his journals. As David obeyed God's call to missions, he journaled his difficulties, battles, and victories daily.

Truth Verse(s): I Corinthians 1:27 and II Corinthians 12:10

Day 68: Bible Discussion

Bible Truth: God uses the weak to reflect his power and strength.

Truth Verse(s): I Corinthians 1:27 and II Corinthians 12:10

Bible Story: I Kings 17:8-16

God told Elijah to go to Zarephath. In Zarephath was a widow woman that God commanded to sustain Elijah. The widow woman was weak in different ways. Being a widow, she had no husband to care for or support her. She was poor and starving. When Elijah found her, he asked her to fetch him some water. She did. Elijah then asked her to bring him some bread. She responded that she had not much food, only a small bit of meal which she was preparing for her and her son to eat, and then die. Elijah told her to fear not and do as he said. Make cakes for him first and then for her and her son. The widow woman did as Elijah had asked and she received a great reward as a result. Her barrel of meal and her cruse of oil would never again run empty until God would send rain to ease the drought and famine.

Just as the widow woman was weak in many ways, so was David. Both trusted what God had called and commanded in their lives. As a result, they were used greatly for the kingdom of God.

Thought: Is there a weakness in your life that God is trying to use for his glory? Give it over to Him.

Day 69: David Brainerd part 3

Bible Truth: Only through faith in Jesus Christ can you be saved.

David Brainerd, as sick as he was, went in God's strength and not in his own. David learned that nothing is impossible with God. But he was not always a Christian.

David grew up in a home with Puritan parents who taught him about God. But most of David's childhood and young adult years were spent working to earn God's favor, as he was not yet a believer in Jesus Christ. David tried to always do what was right and stay away from the wrong crowd. David read Isaiah 64:6, "But we are all as an unclean thing, and all our righteousnesses are as filthy rags". This verse caused a problem for David since he had been trying to earn God's favor through his own righteousness. David kept reading the Bible, terrified of dying and going to hell.

Soon, David realized his works could not save him and only trusting in the completed work of Jesus Christ on the cross could bring one to a saving relationship with God. David called upon Jesus to save him when he was 21 years old. David, now filled with joy through the Holy Spirit, dedicated his life to be used for the glory of God.

God was calling him into the ministry and David responded by enrolling at Yale University. His trials would follow as he pursued the call of Christ in his life.

Truth Verse(s): Ephesians 2:8-9 and Titus 3:5-6

Day 70: Bible Discussion

Bible Truth: Only through faith in Jesus Christ can you be saved.

Truth Verse(s): Ephesians 2:8-9 and Titus 3:5-6

Bible Story: Luke 23:32-43

Two male criminals were also crucified with Jesus at Calvary, one on the right hand and one on the left hand of Jesus. Jesus prayed to ask God the Father to forgive the men who were crucifying Him. The crowd began to mock Jesus. The rulers and soldiers soon joined in to mock Him. Lastly, one of the criminals crucified with Him began to rail on Jesus as well. But the other criminal rebuked Him that mocked Jesus. He said that they justly receive their reward for their crimes, but Jesus was innocent. He admitted by his own words that he was guilty. Then he said to Jesus, "remember me when thou comest into thy kingdom". Jesus responded, "Verily I say unto thee, To day shalt thou be with me in paradise".

Just as the criminal on the cross was guilty, David Brainerd found himself guilty before God. And just as the criminal on the cross could not do anything to earn salvation as He hung on a cross to die, David realized he could not earn salvation either. Just as the criminal asked God to save him that day, David Brainerd called upon Jesus to save him too.

Thought: Do you see yourself as a guilty sinner? Has there been a time in your life that you called upon Jesus and His finished work on the cross to save you?

Day 71: David Brainerd part 4

Bible Truth: When we delight in God, God gives us the desires of our heart.

David was in Yale College studying to be an ordained minister. Before he graduated though, David found himself kicked out of college. David had spoken out against some of the religious teachers at the school and they were not fond of what he had to say. David thought his hopes of becoming a preacher were now slipping away. Little did he know, God had different plans for ministry in David's life. God called David to be a missionary, living in a tent among the savage Indian tribes in the provinces in and around New Jersey. This was a very difficult life for David due to his illness.

David delighted himself in the Lord. David was a prayer warrior, spending time with God, oftentimes, all day. He would write in his journal about his mission work with the Indians, his struggles and victories, and how the Lord encouraged and directed his paths. These journals of David are still used today to encourage modern day Christians in their walk and work for the Lord.

David kept open communication with God through prayer and fasting. As David delighted himself in the Lord, God gave David the desire, not only to share the gospel with the Indians, but brought it to pass as well.

Truth Verse(s): Psalm 37:4-5

Day 72: Bible Discussion

Bible Truth: When we delight in God, God gives us the desires of our heart.
Truth Verse(s): Psalm 37:4-5
Bible Story: Nehemiah 1:3-6 and Nehemiah 2:1-6

Nehemiah was given the sad news about the wall of Jerusalem that had been broken and burned. This broke Nehemiah's heart. Nehemiah knew who to cry out to for help. Nehemiah seeks God through prayer and fasting. He begs God to hear his cry and be attentive to his prayer.

Nehemiah was the cup bearer for the king who held the Israelites captive. Nehemiah's countenance was sad, and the king took notice. He asked Nehemiah what was wrong, and again Nehemiah resorted to prayer. Through Nehemiah's prayer and fasting, God had given him a desire to see the wall of Jerusalem rebuilt. So, Nehemiah made a request to the king to be allowed to return to Jerusalem to rebuild the wall of his home country. God knew Nehemiah delighted in the Lord and heard his prayer. God moved the king's heart to not only allow Nehemiah to return to Jerusalem to rebuild the wall but also provided the timber that would be used to rebuild the gates and walls of Jerusalem as needed.

Nehemiah delighted himself in the Lord through prayer and fasting just like David. As God gave them both desires for the work of the Lord, He also made a way to bring it to pass.

Thought: Are you spending time in prayer to align your desires with God's desires? What desires might He lay on your heart?

Day 73: David Brainerd part 5

Bible Truth: God hears the cry and prayers of the righteous.

David was a prayer warrior. And that's just what the Indians saw that dark but calm night when they surrounded David's tent. They had followed him back to his tent with the intention to kill him. As they watched David in his tent that night, they saw him on bended knee praying. David was hard at work in prayer and God was working on David's behalf to protect him and make a way to soften the Indians' hearts to the gospel.

As David continued in prayer, the Indians watched in quiet astonishment as a rattlesnake slithered into the tent. David was deep in prayer as the deadly rattlesnake slithered closer and closer. As the Indians watched, the snake stood up in striking position towards David, flickering its tongue at David. The Indians watched cautiously assuming the snake would do the job they came to do that night. All of a sudden... nothing! The snake slithered away. The Indians no longer wanted to kill David They knew the power of God and His protection was upon David since the snake did not bite him.

The Indians were willing to listen to the gospel. They listened intently to what David had to say. He explained their sin problem and that Jesus died on the cross to forgive sins. David told them about the new life they could have in Christ and how only He can save their soul and make a home in heaven!

Truth verse(s): Psalm 145:18-19 and Proverbs 15:29

Day 74: Bible Discussion

Bible Truth: God hears the cry and prayers of the righteous.

Truth Verse(s): Psalm 145:18-19 and Proverbs 15:29

Bible Story: II Chronicles 20:1-9, 14-18, 21-24

King Jehoshaphat was advised that Moab and Ammon were coming to battle against him and his people. He feared this information but set himself to pray and seek God for help. As King Jehoshaphat and Judah gathered themselves together to ask for help from the Lord, the Spirit of the Lord fell upon Mattaniah. Mattaniah spoke on behalf of the Lord to not be afraid or dismayed for the battle belongs to God. Furthermore, it was told King Jehoshaphat that Judah would not need to fight either, that God would fight for them.

The day of battle came and as Judah went forth to battle singing praises and worshipping God, the Lord set an ambush on Moab, Ammon, and Mount Seir. They were in a state of confusion and turned on each other instead of Judah and destroyed each other. Just as the Lord said, Judah did not even have to fight.

Just like the Lord fought for David during his prayer, to protect him in that tent against those Indians, God did the same for King Jehoshaphat and Judah. He heard their cries and protected them, working on their behalf. And as God used an interesting tactic to save David through a rattlesnake, He did the same when He gave King Jehoshaphat a victory in the battle without ever fighting. God shows up to fight for His people, His way.

Thought: What battle does God want you to let Him fight in your life?

John Bunyan

Preacher and Best-Selling Author

Day 75: John Bunyan Part 1

Bible Truth: Good fruit can only be produced by a good tree.

It's best to start at the beginning with John. His story reflects the truth found in John 16:33, "These things I have spoken unto you, that in me ye might have peace, In the world ye shall have tribulation: but be of good cheer; I have overcome the world".

John lived in England. He was a troublemaker from a very young age. John was a bully who used foul language, he was disrespectful, disobedient and a thief. One day, his father caught him in a fight and sent him to his room. His father told him to clean up his language and focus on his chores. John promised his dad he would do better but before his dad returned to the bedroom, John had snuck out the window.

John made a small effort to learn about God. He was trying in his own power to be good; to be a better person. But it was not working. On the outside, he looked better, but on the inside, his heart was the same old sinner.

Salvation and a relationship with God were not something that John was going to be able to earn. It can only be a free gift. Ephesians 2:8-9 says, "For by grace ye are saved through faith; and that not of yourselves: it is the gift of God: Not of works, lest any man should boast". John's attempt at good works was getting him nowhere fast.

Truth verses: Luke 6:43-45 and Proverbs 20:11

Day 76: Bible Discussion

Bible Truth: Good fruit can only be produced by a good tree.

Truth Verse(s): Luke 6:43-45 and Proverbs 20:11

Bible Story: Matthew 7:15-23

Matthew records in his gospel how Christians need to be on guard against false prophets that look like sheep but are really wolves. A wolf disguised as a sheep would be difficult to pick out. However, Matthew instructs us that we will be able to see the difference based on works.

A good tree brings forth good fruit. A good tree is not able to bring forth bad fruit. Just the same, a bad tree can only produce corrupt fruit and will not yield good fruit. You will know a true believer by the fruit they produce in their lives. There will be times we slip up and fall into sin even after salvation. However, as a Christian, our good fruits should far outweigh the bad fruit.

Matthew, under the inspiration of the Holy Spirit, continues to write that there will be those in the day of the Lord's return who think they are saved because they are trusting in their own works for salvation and not a relationship with God through faith in the works of Jesus Christ. The saddest verses in all the Bible appear in Matthew 7:21-23.

Even Luke writing under the inspiration of God tells us to bring forth fruits worthy of repentance. It is clear, that good fruit will only be produced when your heart is changed through Jesus.

Thought: Is the fruit in your life sweet or sour?

Day 77: John Bunyan Part 2

Bible Truth: To see heaven, you must repent and be born again.

By the time John was a teenager, he was a lot of things. But most of all, he was a sinner like you and me. We may not have done all the things John did, but sin is sin regardless of how we categorize it as big or small. John's sinful behavior continued from his teenage years into his young adulthood. It was often said of John, "If it weren't for people like John, the devil would have no company in hell".

Hell is a real place where you don't want to spend eternity. The Bible says in Matthew 25:41 and Luke 13:28 that hell is an everlasting fire with weeping and gnashing of teeth. Hell was prepared for the devil and his fallen angels. Hell will be the eternal home for those who have not repented of their sin.

The thought of hell terrified John. He often had bad dreams and nightmares of hell that seemed so real to him. John knew that he was heading down the wide path that led to the gates of hell. He knew he needed to make a change and decided to do something about it.

In 1645 John joined the army. Surely that is a noble, good thing to do. John still did not realize that his good works, even his best works, were not fit to save him from hell.

Truth verse(s): Romans 3:10 and Isaiah 64:6

Day 78: Bible Discussion

Bible Truth: To see heaven, you must repent and be born again.

Truth Verse(s): Romans 3:10 and Isaiah 64:6

Bible Story: John 3:1-21

Nicodemus was a Pharisee, a ruler of the Jews. He knew the OT law very well and lived a very righteous life in his own power. Nicodemus had heard of Jesus and decided to visit him by night. He did not want to be seen by others. Nicodemus knew that Jesus had to come from God because of the miracles done. Then, Jesus told Nicodemus truth that would change his world.

Jesus told Nicodemus that a man must be born again, or he would not see the kingdom of God; heaven as we know it. This confused Nicodemus very much because he spent his whole life learning the law and practicing the law to the best of his ability. Nicodemus asked how this can be. Can one climb back into his mother's womb and be born again a second time? Jesus responded that our first natural birth is flesh born of the flesh. Romans 5:12 explains that the natural man is born in sin and as a result death follows. Jesus continued speaking to Nicodemus and told him that which is born of the Sprit is spirit.

Nicodemus was confused about how one can be born a second time. Jesus responded that Nicodemus is a master of Israel and should know these things. Then Jesus expounded on the greatest gift of everlasting life. He said those who believe in Him will not perish or face condemnation but have eternal life.

Thought: Have you repented of your sins, trusting in Jesus alone?

Day 79: John Bunyan Part 3

Bible Truth: Jesus has power to turn a sinner to a saint.

It wasn't long after joining the army that John was sent off to war. It was during the war, on the battlefield, that John started to see God's protection on his life. John was given orders to help in a siege. Before he left, someone asked to trade places with him. That soldier who traded places with John was shot and killed in battle. He then realized that both good and bad people alike will die and will face their maker. John had a problem still. He was not prepared to meet his Maker.

John fought in the army for a few years. After serving in the army, he married and had a daughter named Mary, who was blind. His wife was a Christian and had brought two Christian books with her when she married John. Sometimes John tried to read them. Other times, his wife nudged him to come to Sunday service. John even felt conviction every now and then when he ignored the tug of God on his heart. He was still terrified of facing God's judgment and hell.

As he walked to work one day, he overheard a group of women talking about their salvation in Jesus through faith. The women invited John to meet their minister, Mr. Gifford. John was surprised that Preacher Gifford had once been as wicked as himself. The time finally came that John laid down his burden at the foot of the cross for salvation. At the age of twenty-five, John became a believer in Jesus Christ and his name was written in the lamb's book of life!

Truth verse(s): John 1:12 and I Timothy 1:15

Day 80: Bible Discussion

Bible Truth: Jesus has power to turn a sinner to a saint.

Truth Verse(s): John 1:12 and Acts 26:15-18

Bible Story: Luke 19:1-10

As Jesus traveled, He entered and passed through the town of Jericho. News of Jesus spread, and people were eager to get a glimpse of him. There was a "wee little man" named Zacchaeus who lived in Jericho. He held a high position among the publicans and was very wealthy. Publicans in Jesus's time were known to steal and take advantage of the poor for their own benefit. They were not very much liked by the people.

Zacchaeus climbed a sycamore tree to see Jesus as He passed by his way. Jesus took note of Zacchaeus. It may seem as though Zacchaeus was looking for Jesus that day, but truth be told, it was the other way around. Jesus had his eye on Zacchaeus.

Jesus told Zacchaeus to hurry down from the tree as He intended to abide at Zacchaeus' house. Those in the crowd murmured and complained that Jesus was going to be the guest of a sinner.

Zacchaeus was overcome with guilt and shame, just like John Bunyan. Zacchaeus turned to Jesus that day for salvation and changed his ways making right his prior wrongs. Jesus exclaimed that He had come to seek and save the lost. Just like Jesus sought out Zacchaeus, Jesus sought out John Bunyan. Both were made new in Christ and became the sons of God.

Thought: Are you a sinner turned saint through the power of Jesus? Is He convicting your heart to change something?

Day 81: John Bunyan Part 4

Bible Truth: God gives us courage and strength to obey God and not fear man, even when facing persecution.

John changed his life completely for God. In the 1600's, only those who were ordained by the church of England were allowed to preach God's word. But that didn't stop the tinker by trade and John became a preacher of the gospel.

John's wife died after giving birth to their fourth child, and life was difficult for John. He remarried a Christian lady named Elizabeth. Elizabeth asked John if he would preach from the approved 'King's Book of Common Prayer'? John said no, he only intended to preach out of God's book, the Bible.

One Sunday morning, news reached John that a warrant was put out for his arrest for preaching against the king's commandments. They urged John to cancel the service, but John refused. He would not allow the fear of man to dictate his obedience to preach God's word. That service was interrupted, and John was arrested.

John spent a couple of months in prison before he was called to answer his charges. John told them, even if he was released from prison that day, he would not stop preaching God's word! John wanted to obey God rather than man. He feared God, not man. And as a result, John spent years in prison.

Truth verse(s): John 16:33, II Timothy 1:7, and Matthew 10:28

Day 82: Bible Discussion

Bible Truth: God gives us courage and strength to obey God and not fear man, even when facing persecution.

Truth Verse(s): John 16:33, II Timothy 1:7, and Matthew 10:28

Bible Story: Acts 5:17-32

The high priest and other leaders of the Sadducees were angry that the apostles were preaching Jesus to the people in Jerusalem. The Jewish leaders did not believe in Jesus and only wanted the people to follow how they interpreted God's word. This was similar to the church of England during John's time where people had to follow the books given by the king and not the Bible. The Jewish leaders laid hands on these apostles and put them in prison for preaching Jesus Christ.

At night, an angel of the Lord opened the prison doors and freed the apostles. The angel instructed them to go back to the temple in the city of Jerusalem and speak the words of life to the people again. This was the same act that got them arrested the first time. Nevertheless, they obeyed God's instructions.

The next morning, the leaders called to have the apostles brought from prison, only to find, the prisoners were gone. The apostles were found in the city preaching Jesus again. The captain of the officers brought the men to the Jewish leaders and asked them, "Did we not straitly command you that ye should not teach in this name"? Peter responded that they would obey God rather than man.

Thought: Is there an area of your life you have yet to obey God in because you fear man

94

Day 83: John Bunyan Part 5

Bible Truth: God uses trials in our life to get glory, conform us to the image of Christ, and work out his good plan.

John spent twelve years in prison for preaching God's word and truth about Jesus Christ and salvation. Why would God allow that to happen to John when he only sought to teach the truths of God's word? John often prayed to God. He trusted that God had a good plan through all of this. John took to making leather laces to help support his wife and children as well as writing books. The longer he stayed in prison, the better his books sold. John wrote over 60 books, mostly while in prison.

It was during John's time in prison that John had dreams that seemed so real. And out of these dreams John wrote one of the best-selling books of all time, 'Pilgrim's Progress'. This is the story of Pilgrim, who had a heavy burden and longed to know God and reach the Celestial City. During Pilgrim's journey to find truth and know God, he faces many challenges and enemies along the way that try to sidetrack and discourage Pilgrim. Pilgrim keeps fighting against the enemy until he reaches the Celestial City. This book is an allegory depicting the life of a Christian fighting against the wiles of the devil. This is a book that has encouraged millions to search for truth. 'Pilgrim's Progress' has helped countless Christians press on towards the kingdom of God during their own journey as a pilgrim in this world.

Truth verse(s): James 1:2-4 and I Peter 1:6-7

Day 84: Bible Discussion

Bible Truth: God uses trials in our life to get glory and work out his good plan.

Truth Verse(s): James 1:2-4 and I Peter 1:6-7

Bible Story: John 11:1-7, 11-15, 17, 23-26, 34-35, 39-44

Jesus was a few days journey away from Judaea, where his friends Mary, Martha, and Lazarus lived, when he heard that Lazarus was sick. Jesus stated that the sickness was for the glory of God. After two days of receiving the news, Jesus departed to Judaea.

Jesus explained that Lazarus was dead and when Jesus arrived in Judaea, Lazurus had been in the grave four days. It was very sad for Mary and Martha. Jesus told Martha that Lazarus, her brother, will rise again. God's goal was to show the people that Jesus is the true resurrection and life, even over death.

Jesus asked where they laid Lazarus' body. Then, Jesus commanded them to remove the stone of the tomb. Jesus cried in a loud voice for Lazarus to come forth from the grave and dead Lazarus came back to life!

Just as God used this trial in the life of Mary and Martha, God used the trials and difficulty of twelve years in prison to

accomplish a far greater plan with John Bunyan. God is still using John Bunyan today to build up believers in their pilgrimage to the Celestial City, heaven.

Thought: Is there a trial in your life that you God desires to use for his glory and for the edifying of others?

Day 85: Final Thoughts

The title of this devotional book was taken from both the Old Testament and New Testament scripture. Romans 10:14-15 says, "How then shall they call on Him in whom they have not believed? and how shall they believe in Him of whom they have not heard? and how shall they hear without a preacher? And how shall they preach, except they be sent? as it is written, How beautiful are the feet of them that preach the gospel of peace, and bring glad tidings of good things"! Isaiah 52:7 says, "How beautiful upon the mountains are the feet of him that bringeth good tidings, that publisheth peace; that bringeth good tidings of good, that publisheth salvation; that saith unto Zion, Thy God reigneth"!

God desires to use our lives, even though we are not on the far away mission field but right here in our local Jerusalem. He wants to get glory and work out his perfect plan to accomplish, not only his will for our lives, but to use us to bring others to the foot of the cross. We can learn a lot from these stories and great heroes of the faith. The simple lessons and Biblical principles that can be seen through the lives and stories of these individuals can also be gleaned by us and lived out in our lives today. Are you ready for your feet to have an impact on the lost and dying world around you? Let's not allow the name of God to be blasphemed among a lost and dying world because our feet do not carry the beautiful things of God. Rather, let's be a sweet-smelling savor for all to see God's glory in our lives.

Thought: Are your feet being used for the beautiful things of God, to bring people to Christ, or turning them away?

Honorable Mentions

I dedicate this book to my husband, John Clemento, who continued to encourage me to take my vacation Bible school stories and put them in a book to encourage families in their family devotion time. I also dedicate this to my children, Madelyn, Joslyn, and John, who not only heard these stories as they attended VBS, but also gave me time to work on this book at home.

Thanks to my church, Open Bible Baptist Church who has a great vision for missions and gave the opportunity to teach these stories to many children.

A special thanks to both John and Mrs. Sandy Wilson for helping with edits in the draft stage.

Most of all, thanks to my Lord and Savior Jesus Christ who saved my life and made me new! Without Him, none of this would be possible.

I learn best through stories and I hope that you will find this devotional book a great way to inter-twine missionary stories and scripture.

Author Biography

Stacey Clemento is a born-again Christian, saved by the grace of Jesus Christ in 2004. She is happily married to John, her high school sweetheart, and serves alongside him in several of the children's ministries at their local church, where they have been attending since 2009. Together, they are raising three children: two daughters and a son. Stacey teaches secondary education at a local Christian school. She earned her B.A. in Business Administration at Liberty University in 2020.

John & Stacey

www.ingramcontent.com/pod-product-compliance
Lightning Source LLC
Chambersburg PA
CBHW072345220125
20519CB00008B/160